P9-CLX-770

Para Elizabeth

Publicado originalmente en 2009 por Walker Books Limited

Título original: *¿Where's Wally? The Incredible Paper Chase*

Traducción: Laura Paredes

1.ª edición: mayo, 2012

Martin Handford ha establecido su derecho a ser identificado
como el autor/ilustrador de esta obra

© 1990, 1991, 2009 Martin Handford

© 2012, Ediciones B, S.A.,
en español para todo el mundo
Consell de Cent, 425-427 – 08009 Barcelona (España)
www.edicionesb.com
ISBN: 978-84-666-4996-4

Ésta es una coedición de Ediciones B, S. A.,
con Walker Books Ltd.

Printed in China - Impreso en China

¿DÓNDE ESTÁ WALLY?
EN BUSCA DE LA NOTA PERDIDA

MARTIN HANDFORD

EDICIONES B
GRUPO ZETA

Barcelona • Bogotá • Buenos Aires • Caracas • Madrid • México D. F. • Montevideo • Quito • Santiago de Chile

¿DÓNDE ESTÁ WALLY?
RETOS DE EN BUSCA DE LA NOTA PERDIDA

ASALTO AL CASTILLO

- [ ] 5 soldados azules con penachos azules
- [ ] 5 soldados rojos con penachos rojos
- [ ] 1 soldado azul con un penacho rojo
- [ ] 1 soldado rojo con un penacho azul
- [ ] 4 arqueros azules
- [ ] 5 personajes sujetando una pluma blanca
- [ ] Soldados con picas
- [ ] Menores excavando un túnel
- [ ] 22 escaleras de mano
- [ ] Soldados con arcos rectos
- [ ] 5 catapultas y 3 tirachinas
- [ ] 27 damas vestidas de azul
- [ ] 12 hombres con barba blanca
- [ ] 1 pozo de los deseos
- [ ] 2 brujas aseadas
- [ ] 9 escudos azules
- [ ] 4 caballos
- [ ] 3 escudos redondos de color rojo
- [ ] 1 prisionero en una postura desconcertante
- [ ] 8 hombres echando una cabezada
- [ ] Alguien con el pelo larguísimo
- [ ] 1 soldado con un pie descalzo
- [ ] 18 personajes que sacan la lengua
- [ ] 5 tiendas

JUEGOS JURÁSICOS

- [ ] Un partido de voleibol
- [ ] Una regata
- [ ] Dinosaurios jugando al críquet
- [ ] Un partido de fútbol
- [ ] Una carrera de windsurfistas
- [ ] Dinosaurios jugando al béisbol
- [ ] Un partido de fútbol americano
- [ ] Dinosaurios jugando al baloncesto
- [ ] Dinosaurios jugando al golf
- [ ] Una carrera de obstáculos
- [ ] Un partido de polo
- [ ] 4 grupos de animadoras
- [ ] Colas convertidas en marcadores
- [ ] Un concurso hípico de saltos

RETRATADOS

- [ ] 1 pájaro que voló del marco
- [ ] 1 dragón enfadado
- [ ] 1 avión con alas de verdad
- [ ] 1 despertador
- [ ] 1 cactus corriendo
- [ ] 1 tronco de árbol descarado
- [ ] Unos dedos de pescado
- [ ] 1 sirena al revés
- [ ] 3 esquiadores
- [ ] Alguien que come sin modales
- [ ] 1 retrato cabeza abajo
- [ ] 1 pie enorme
- [ ] 3 animales románticos
- [ ] 1 pie víctima de las cosquillas
- [ ] 1 retrato dentro de otro retrato
- [ ] 2 hombres unidos por el sombrero
- [ ] 2 cascos puestos del revés
- [ ] Alguien que bebe con una pajita
- [ ] 3 banderas
- [ ] 9 lenguas fuera
- [ ] 1 cavernícola fuera de su marco
- [ ] 7 perros y 1 perro de agua
- [ ] 1 dedo vendado
- [ ] 1 bigote trenzado
- [ ] 4 barbas
- [ ] 3 cascos con penacho rojo
- [ ] 4 gatos
- [ ] 4 patos
- [ ] 1 marco amarillo, 1 azul y 1 rojo

¡RETIRADA!

- [ ] 1 escudo que se vacía de golpe
- [ ] 1 corazón en la túnica de un soldado
- [ ] 1 espada curvada
- [ ] 1 soldado con un martillo
- [ ] 1 lanza rayada
- [ ] 1 soldado con el torso desnudo
- [ ] 2 botas fugitivas
- [ ] 1 jinete sin caballo
- [ ] 1 soldado con una espada y un hacha
- [ ] 3 pies descalzos
- [ ] 4 colas rosas
- [ ] 1 lanza con puntas en ambos lados
- [ ] 1 casco con penacho azul
- [ ] 1 soldado con una bota roja y otra azul
- [ ] 1 casco con penacho rojo

EL JUEGO DE LA SELVA

- [ ] 1 explorador con manga larga
- [ ] 1 explorador con dos lanzas
- [ ] 1 explorador con un pie calzado
- [ ] 4 ranas satisfechas
- [ ] 1 explorador con barba blanca
- [ ] 5 exploradores con el torso desnudo
- [ ] 1 dedo víctima de un mordisco
- [ ] 1 explorador con una serpiente enroscada
- [ ] 1 hebilla de cinturón en la espalda
- [ ] 1 explorador con dos bandoleras
- [ ] 10 mariposas
- [ ] 1 lanza con puntas en ambos lados
- [ ] 8 exploradores que señalan y ríen
- [ ] 3 lanzas rotas

¡DÍA DE PERROS!

- [ ] 1 soldado perro de caza
- [ ] 1 soldado perro guardián
- [ ] 1 soldado perro de pelea
- [ ] 1 soldado sabueso
- [ ] 1 soldado gran danés
- [ ] 1 soldado caniche
- [ ] 2 soldados pidiendo un hueso
- [ ] 2 soldados en pos de una pelota
- [ ] 4 estrellas en una túnica
- [ ] 1 cesta para perro
- [ ] 1 perro con máscara de hombre
- [ ] 2 del mismo bando peleándose
- [ ] 4 pies con cosquillas
- [ ] 1 soldado aullando
- [ ] 1 soldado con dos rabos
- [ ] 1 estrella blanca en una túnica crema
- [ ] Ojos crema en una máscara blanca
- [ ] 1 hombre con una pierna negra y otra marrón
- [ ] 1 hombre con un brazo negro y otro crema
- [ ] 1 manga a rayas azules y guante crema
- [ ] 1 manga a rayas negras y guante crema
- [ ] 1 máscara marrón con una túnica azul
- [ ] 1 nariz azul en una máscara marrón

REDOBLE DE TAMBOR

- [ ] Una fila trasera muy descarada
- [ ] Un saludo que provoca un choque
- [ ] Unas lanzas cortísimas
- [ ] 1 grupo mirando en todas direcciones
- [ ] Un choque a punto de ocurrir
- [ ] Un reacción en cadena
- [ ] Lanzas cabeza abajo
- [ ] 1 lanza interminable
- [ ] 2 sombreros unidos
- [ ] Unos soldados muy desaliñados
- [ ] 1 soldado con un solo zapato
- [ ] 1 soldado con zapatos rojos
- [ ] 35 caballos
- [ ] 1 cinta de sombrero rosa y otra azul
- [ ] 1 lanza azul
- [ ] 1 zapato perdido
- [ ] 1 sombrero con penacho amarillo
- [ ] 1 sombrero con una cinta roja

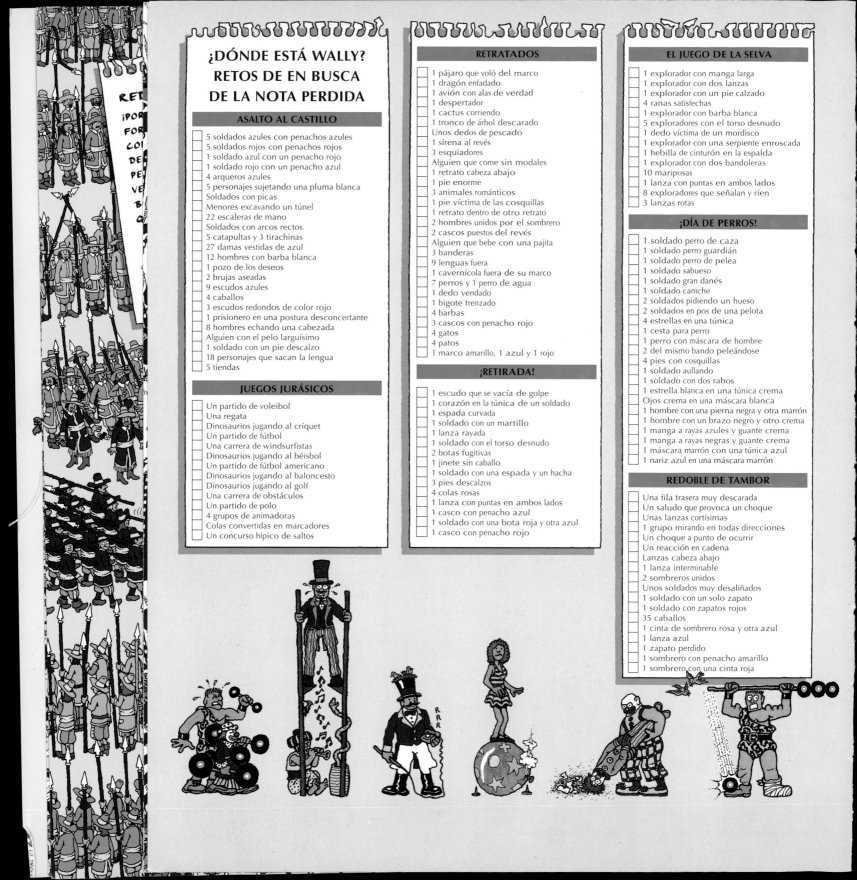

LA ESCAPADA

- [ ] 10 hombres con capucha verde
- [ ] 10 hombres con un solo guante
- [ ] 10 encapuchados con guantes de otro color
- [ ] 10 hombres con guantes de distinto color
- [ ] 10 hombres con un guante largo y otro corto
- [ ] 10 guantes perdidos
- [ ] 10 hombres con un mitón
- [ ] 6 escaleras de mano
- [ ] 19 palas
- [ ] 5 interrogantes formados por el seto

LA GRAN FIESTA

- [ ] 5 cabezas de Wally vistas desde detrás
- [ ] Una reverencia hacia atrás
- [ ] 2 forzudos ignorados
- [ ] 1 banda de ocho hombres
- [ ] 1 neumático pinchado
- [ ] 1 casco puesto del revés
- [ ] 8 ruedas delanteras
- [ ] 2 caras de Wally cabeza abajo
- [ ] 1 motorista sin moto
- [ ] 7 botas rojas
- [ ] 1 hombre envuelto en una serpentina
- [ ] 1 uniforme demasiado pequeño
- [ ] 1 uniforme demasiado grande
- [ ] 2 hombres en una sola moto
- [ ] Alguien con corbata roja
- [ ] Alguien con boina azul
- [ ] 1 reposabrazos reacio

EL DELIRANTE CIRCO WALLY

- [ ] 4 Hombres bala reacios
- [ ] 1 payaso con cinco sombreros
- [ ] 1 payaso con una gran narizota
- [ ] 1 músico que no deshizo la maleta
- [ ] 1 familia de cuatro miembros con gafas
- [ ] 1 pajarita en el pelo de un payaso
- [ ] 1 gélido vendedor de polos
- [ ] 1 hombre que sostiene a tres
- [ ] 3 pajitas en un vaso
- [ ] 2 payasos sedientos
- [ ] 1 payaso que sirve de escoba
- [ ] 3 víctimas del ketchup
- [ ] 1 chico con tres bebidas
- [ ] 1 hombre con seis vasos
- [ ] 12 payasos con flores en el sombrero

LA GRAN FIESTA – SOLUCIÓN

1 Francia	10 Suiza	**BANDERAS CON FALLOS**
2 Países Bajos	11 Estados Unidos	3 Faltan las rayas rojas diagonales
3 Reino Unido	12 Canadá	4 Ondea cabeza abajo
4 Suecia	13 Bélgica	5 Falta una estrella
5 Australia	14 Nueva Zelanda	11 Rayas roja y blanca al revés
6 Noruega	15 Finlandia	12 Hoja de arce cabeza abajo
7 España	16 Austria	14 Faltan las rayas rojas diagonales
8 Japón	17 Alemania	
9 Dinamarca	18 Brasil	

LÁPIZ Y PAPEL

¿Encontraste la hoja de papel que Wally dejó en cada una de las escenas? Wally también dejó el lápiz en algún punto del trayecto, ¿podéis regresar a buscarlo, superbuscadores?

¡Y DOS COSAS MÁS!

En este libro aparecen muchos imitawallys (por lo menos uno en cada escena, ¡pero muchos más en algunas!).

Hay un personaje femenino además de Wally, Woof, Wenda, Barbablanca y Odlaw en cada escena. ¡Búscalo!

¡VENGAN, SEÑORES, VENGAN!
¡Pasen y vean!
¡Diversión garantizada!

¡El delirante Circo Wally
ha llegado a la ciudad!

EL DELIRANTE CIRCO WALLY
¡DIVIÉRTETE CON LAS PRÓXIMAS
PÁGINAS! DESPLIÉGALAS Y RECORTA
LOS ACRÓBATAS, LOS PAYASOS
Y LOS TITIRITEROS... PARA MONTAR
EL CIRCO, MIRA EL INTERIOR DEL
SOBRE. INVITA A TUS AMIGOS,
PARIENTES Y MASCOTAS. ¡CUANTOS
MÁS, MEJOR! ¡Y QUE SUENE LA
FANFARRIA! ¡REPARTE LAS PALOMITAS
Y MONTA TU PROPIO ESPECTÁCULO!
¡GENIAL!

DATE DUE

NOV 30 '90			
NOV 30 '90	NOV 30 '91	OCT 21 '9	
NOV 30 '91	FEB 28 '92	JAN 6	
NOV 22 '91	DEC 7 '92	JAN 25	
NOV 30 '91	DEC 18 '92	JAN 26	
DEC 18 '91	JAN 8 '93		
	1/14		
DEC 18 '91	DEC 10 '93	DE 15 '00	
JAN 10 '92	DEC 10 '93		
JAN 31 '92	DEC 10 '93		

THE
CROW

THE
CROW

Frederick E. Hoxie

D'Arcy McNickle Center for the History of the American Indian,
Newberry Library

Frank W. Porter III
General Editor

CHELSEA HOUSE PUBLISHERS
New York   Philadelphia

9703
Ho-1
10/90 H

On the cover A 19th-century rawhide shield owned by
Crow Indian Wraps Up His Tail

Chelsea House Publishers
Editor-in-Chief Nancy Toff
Executive Editor Remmel T. Nunn
Managing Editor Karyn Gullen Brown
Copy Chief Juliann Barbato
Picture Editor Adrian G. Allen
Art Director Maria Epes
Manufacturing Manager Gerald Levine

Indians of North America
Senior Editor Liz Sonneborn

Staff for **THE CROW**
Deputy Copy Chief Nicole Bowen
Editorial Assistant Claire M. Wilson
Assistant Art Director Loraine Machlin
Designer Donna Sinisgalli
Designer Assistant James Baker
Picture Researcher Anne Bohlen
Production Coordinator Joseph Romano

First Printing

1 3 5 7 9 8 6 4 2 8

Library of Congress Cataloging-in-Publication Data

Hoxie, Frederick E., 1947–
The Crow / Frederick E. Hoxie
    p.   cm.—(Indians of North America)
Bibliography: p.
Includes index.
Summary: Examines the culture, history, and changing
fortunes of the Crow Indians.
ISBN 1-55546-704-0
        0-7910-0379-5 (pbk.)
1. Crow Indians—Juvenile literature. 2. Indians of North
America—Great Plains—Juvenile literature. [1. Crow
Indians.   2. Indians of North America—Great Plains.] I. Title.
II. Series: Indians of North America (Chelsea House   89-964
Publishers)   CIP
E99.C92H68   1989   AC

CONTENTS

INDIANS OF NORTH AMERICA

The Abenaki

American Indian
   Literature

The Apache

The Arapaho

The Archaeology
   of North America

The Aztecs

The Cahuilla

The Catawbas

The Cherokee

The Cheyenne

The Chickasaw

The Chinook

The Chipewyan

The Choctaw

The Chumash

The Coast Salish Peoples

The Comanche

The Creek

The Crow

The Eskimo

Federal Indian Policy

The Hidatsa

The Huron

The Iroquois

The Kiowa

The Kwakiutl

The Lenapes

The Lumbee

The Maya

The Menominee

The Modoc

The Montagnais-Naskapi

The Nanticoke

The Narragansett

The Navajo

The Nez Perce

The Ojibwa

The Osage

The Paiute

The Pima-Maricopa

The Potawatomi

The Powhatan Tribes

The Pueblo

The Quapaw

The Seminole

The Tarahumara

The Tunica-Biloxi

Urban Indians

The Wampanoag

Women in American
   Indian Society

The Yakima

The Yankton Sioux

The Yuma

CHELSEA HOUSE PUBLISHERS

INDIANS OF NORTH AMERICA:
CONFLICT AND SURVIVAL

Frank W. Porter III

*The Indians survived our open intention of wiping them out, and
since the tide turned they have even weathered our good intentions
toward them, which can be much more deadly.*

John Steinbeck
America and Americans

When Europeans first reached the North American continent, they found
hundreds of tribes occupying a vast and rich country. The newcomers quickly
recognized the wealth of natural resources. They were not, however, so quick
or willing to recognize the spiritual, cultural, and intellectual riches of the
people they called Indians.

The Indians of North America examines the problems that develop when
people with different cultures come together. For American Indians, the
consequences of their interaction with non-Indian people have been both
productive and tragic. The Europeans believed they had "discovered" a "New
World," but their religious bigotry, cultural bias, and materialistic world view
kept them from appreciating and understanding the people who lived in it.
All too often they attempted to change the way of life of the indigenous
people. The Spanish conquistadores wanted the Indians as a source of labor.
The Christian missionaries, many of whom were English, viewed them as
potential converts. French traders and trappers used the Indians as a means
to obtain pelts. As Francis Parkman, the 19th-century historian, stated, "Spanish civilization crushed the Indian; English civilization scorned and neglected
him; French civilization embraced and cherished him."

Nearly 500 years later, many people think of American Indians as curious vestiges of a distant past, waging a futile war to survive in a Space Age society. Even today, our understanding of the history and culture of American Indians is too often derived from unsympathetic, culturally biased, and inaccurate reports. The American Indian, described and portrayed in thousands of movies, television programs, books, articles, and government studies, has either been raised to the status of the "noble savage" or disparaged as the "wild Indian" who resisted the westward expansion of the American frontier.

Where in this popular view are the real Indians, the human beings and communities whose ancestors can be traced back to ice-age hunters? Where are the creative and indomitable people whose sophisticated technologies used the natural resources to ensure their survival, whose military skill might even have prevented European settlement of North America if not for devastating epidemics and disruption of the ecology? Where are the men and women who are today diligently struggling to assert their legal rights and express once again the value of their heritage?

The various Indian tribes of North America, like people everywhere, have a history that includes population expansion, adaptation to a range of regional environments, trade across wide networks, internal strife, and warfare. This was the reality. Europeans justified their conquests, however, by creating a mythical image of the New World and its native people. In this myth, the New World was a virgin land, waiting for the Europeans. The arrival of Christopher Columbus ended a timeless primitiveness for the original inhabitants.

Also part of this myth was the debate over the origins of the American Indians. Fantastic and diverse answers were proposed by the early explorers, missionairies, and settlers. Some thought that the Indians were descended from the Ten Lost Tribes of Israel, others that they were descended from inhabitants of the lost continent of Atlantis. One writer suggested that the Indians had reached North America in another Noah's ark.

A later myth, perpetrated by many historians, focused on the relentless persecution during the past five centuries until only a scattering of these "primitive" people remained to be herded onto reservations. This view fails to chronicle the overt and covert ways in which the Indians successfully coped with the intruders.

All of these myths presented one-sided interpretations that ignored the complexity of European and American events and policies. All left serious questions unanswered. What were the origins of the American Indians? Where did they come from? How and when did they get to the New World? What was their life—their culture—really like?

In the late 1800s, anthropologists and archaeologists in the Smithsonian Institution's newly created Bureau of American Ethnology in Washington,

D.C., began to study scientifically the history and culture of the Indians of North America. They were motivated by an honest belief that the Indians were on the verge of extinction and that along with them would vanish their languages, religious beliefs, technology, myths, and legends. These men and women went out to visit, study, and record data from as many Indian communities as possible before this information was forever lost.

By this time there was a new myth in the national consciousness. American Indians existed as figures in the American past. They had performed a historical mission. They had challenged white settlers who trekked across the continent. Once conquered, however, they were supposed to accept graciously the way of life of their conquerors.

The reality again was different. American Indians resisted both actively and passively. They refused to lose their unique identity, to be assimilated into white society. Many whites viewed the Indians not only as members of a conquered nation but also as "inferior" and "unequal." The rights of the Indians could be expanded, contracted, or modified as the conquerors saw fit. In every generation, white society asked itself what to do with the American Indians. Their answers have resulted in the twists and turns of federal Indian policy.

There were two general approaches. One way was to raise the Indians to a "higher level" by "civilizing" them. Zealous missionaries considered it their Christian duty to elevate the Indian through conversion and scanty education. The other approach was to ignore the Indians until they disappeared under pressure from the ever-expanding white society. The myth of the "vanishing Indian" gave stronger support to the latter option, helping to justify the taking of the Indians' land.

Prior to the end of the 18th century, there was no national policy on Indians simply because the American nation has not yet come into existence. American Indians similarly did not possess a political or social unity with which to confront the various Europeans. They were not homogeneous. Rather, they were loosely formed bands and tribes, speaking nearly 300 languages and thousands of dialects. The collective identity felt by Indians today is a result of their common experiences of defeat and/or mistreatment at the hands of whites.

During the colonial period, the British crown did not have a coordinated policy toward the Indians of North America. Specific tribes (most notably the Iroquois and the Cherokee) became military and political pawns used by both the crown and the individual colonies. The success of the American Revolution brought no immediate change. When the United States acquired new territory from France and Mexico in the early 19th century, the federal government wanted to open this land to settlement by homesteaders. But the Indian tribes that lived on this land had signed treaties with European governments assuring their title to the land. Now the United States assumed legal responsibility for honoring these treaties.

At first, President Thomas Jefferson believed that the Louisiana Purchase contained sufficient land for both the Indians and the white population. Within a generation, though, it became clear that the Indians would not be allowed to remain. In the 1830s the federal government began to coerce the eastern tribes to sign treaties agreeing to relinquish their ancestral land and move west of the Mississippi River. Whenever these negotiations failed, President Andrew Jackson used the military to remove the Indians. The southeastern tribes, promised food and transportation during their removal to the West, were instead forced to walk the "Trail of Tears." More than 4,000 men, woman, and children died during this forced march. The "removal policy" was successful in opening the land to homesteaders, but it created enormous hardships for the Indians.

By 1871 most of the tribes in the United States had signed treaties ceding most or all of their ancestral land in exchange for reservations and welfare. The treaty terms were intended to bind both parties for all time. But in the General Allotment Act of 1887, the federal government changed its policy again. Now the goal was to make tribal members into individual landowners and farmers, encouraging their absorption into white society. This policy was advantageous to whites who were eager to acquire Indian land, but it proved disastrous for the Indians. One hundred thirty-eight million acres of reservation land were subdivided into tracts of 160, 80, or as little as 40 acres, and allotted tribe members on an individual basis. Land owned in this way was said to have "trust status" and could not be sold. But the surplus land—all Indian land not allotted to individuals—was opened (for sale) to white settlers. Ultimately, more than 90 million acres of land were taken from the Indians by legal and illegal means.

The resulting loss of land was a catastrophe for the Indians. It was necessary to make it illegal for Indians to sell their land to non-Indians. The Indian Reorganization Act of 1934 officially ended the allotment period. Tribes that voted to accept the provisions of this act were reorganized, and an effort was made to purchase land within preexisting reservations to restore an adequate land base.

Ten years later, in 1944, federal Indian policy again shifted. Now the federal government wanted to get out of the "Indian business." In 1953 an act of Congress named specific tribes whose trust status was to be ended "at the earliest possible time." This new law enabled the United States to end unilaterally, whether the Indians wished it or not, the special status that protected the land in Indian tribal reservations. In the 1950s federal Indian policy was to transfer federal responsibility and jurisdiction to state governments, encourage the physical relocation of Indian peoples from reservations to urban areas, and hasten the termination, or extinction, of tribes.

Between 1954 and 1962 Congress passed specific laws authorizing the termination of more than 100 tribal groups. The stated purpose of the termination policy was to ensure the full and complete integration of Indians into American society. However, there is a less benign way to interpret this legislation. Even as termination was being discussed in Congress, 133 separate bills were introduced to permit the transfer of trust land ownership from Indians to non-Indians.

With the Johnson administration in the 1960s the federal government began to reject termination. In the 1970s yet another Indian policy emerged. Known as "self-determination," it favored keeping the protective role of the federal government while increasing tribal participation in, and control of, important areas of local government. In 1983 President Reagan, in a policy statement on Indian affairs, restated the unique "government is government" relationship of the United States with the Indians. However, federal programs since then have moved toward transferring Indian affairs to individual states, which have long desired to gain control of Indian land and resources.

As long as American Indians retain power, land, and resources that are coveted by the states and the federal government, there will continue to be a "clash of cultures," and the issues will be contested in the courts, Congress, the White House, and even in the international human rights community. To give all Americans a greater comprehension of the issues and conflicts involving American Indians today is a major goal of this series. These issues are not easily understood, nor can these conflicts be readily resolved. The study of North American Indian history and culture is a necessary and important step toward that comprehension. All Americans must learn the history of the relations between the Indians and the federal government, recognize the unique legal status of the Indians, and understand the heritage and cultures of the Indians of North America.

Chah-ee-chopes (Four Wolves), painted by American artist George Catlin, who visited the Crow in 1832.

THE
CREATION

Two men, one white and one an elderly Crow Indian, sat together in the summer sunlight. The white man held a notepad in his lap. He had a question.

"Where did your people come from?"

The old Crow, Yellow Brow, nearly laughed. Such a silly question, he thought. But he had agreed to help this stranger who had come to the Crow's Montana homeland to study his people's beliefs. Besides, Yellow Brow took great pride in his knowledge of Crow history. Despite the visitor's simple ways, he would be happy to answer.

Sitting with this white man—University of California anthropology professor Robert Lowie—in 1931, Yellow Brow remembered the winter nights of his childhood. His grandfathers, Good Buffalo Calf and Uses Scalp for a Necklace, would call, "Ikye´!" (Attention!) to gather their families around them to hear a story. That was long ago, when

the buffalo still roamed the Bighorn River valley. Suddenly Yellow Brow was glad this curious visitor had come to interview him. It would be a chance to tell again the story of human creation. "Ikye´!" he called and began:

Old Man Coyote gazed across the water and felt lonely. The sea stretched to the horizon in every direction. "It is bad to be alone," Coyote thought.

As he stretched his neck to scan the endless gray sea, Coyote saw two red-eyed ducks paddling toward him. Eagerly he asked them if they had seen anything in their travels.

The ducks' eyes narrowed, and they looked this way and that. "We haven't actually seen anything, elder brother," the first duck replied. "But deep down in our hearts we have wondered about what lies within the sea."

Coyote was interested. "You both can swim and dive. Why don't you dive under the water and look?" he suggested. "Perhaps there is something down there. If you find something, bring it up, and we will look at it."

One duck stayed with Coyote while his companion dived into the sea. They waited for the little duck to return.

"Oh, my," Coyote exclaimed after several minutes, "my younger brother has probably drowned. He has been gone too long."

"We can stay down a long time," the duck at his side assured him. "Don't worry, our brother will return."

After a long time, the diver returned to the surface. He had something in his mouth. The two who were waiting rushed over to him, eager to see what he was carrying.

"I struck something hard down there," the duck reported.

Coyote examined the object and determined that it was a piece of root or perhaps a branch from a tree.

"Your hearts were right. There is something down there all right," Coyote announced. He turned to the diving duck and said, "Why don't you try again, and this time, try to find something soft. If you do, scoop it up in your bill and bring it back for us to see."

The diving duck agreed and quickly disappeared beneath the surface once more. Again, Coyote began to worry that he had been gone too long, and again, the other duck comforted him. Finally, they saw the diver swimming in their direction.

"Well, how did you make out? Do you have something?" Coyote asked, nearly shouting with excitement.

"Yes," the duck replied. He had a lump of mud.

"Well, my younger brothers," Coyote said, "this is something we can build with."

The ducks were puzzled but they waited as Coyote blew on the mud. Magically, it expanded in every direction and grew deep and firm. Within a few minutes, Coyote had made a large island.

The ducks were amazed. "Elder brother," they squealed, "this is fine. Can you make it bigger?"

Again, Coyote blew on the earth, and again, it grew in all directions. Almost instantly the island became as large as the earth is today.

The three looked around and admired the brown prairie that stretched before them. Finally one of the ducks said absently, "It would be so much nicer if it weren't empty."

Coyote reached down and picked up the root the duck had retrieved from the bottom of the sea. From that little scrap he made the grass, the trees, and all the other plants we find on the earth.

Again, the three stood and admired Coyote's new creation. "It is beautiful," the other duck sighed, "but it's so flat. If there were rivers here, they would dig valleys and cut canyons into the earth."

Coyote scratched his grizzly chin and nodded his head. "You're right," he replied. As the ducks stood in wonder, he pushed the earth around and arranged it so that rivers flowed across the landscape.

Now the ducks glowed with pleasure. "This is perfect," they said. "Who could imagine anything more?"

It was Coyote's turn to be dissatisfied. "This is very beautiful," he agreed. "The grass, the rivers, the trees, and the valleys stretching to the horizon—all of this is good. But I am lonely and bored. We need companions."

Coyote scooped up a handful of earth and shaped it into men. The ducks were fascinated.

"Could you make companions for us?" they asked.

"Of course," Coyote said, and he made ducks of all varieties.

Coyote looked with pleasure at his handiwork until he thought of something he had left out. "If there were women, the men would be content, and they could multiply and grow strong. If there were female ducks, the male ducks, too, would be happy and plentiful." He took another handful of dirt and made women and female ducks.

That is the way it was. The earth was beautiful, and men were happy. Then one day Old Man Coyote met another

Anthropologist Robert Lowie and a companion on the Crow Indian Reservation in 1910.

coyote. "My brother!" he exclaimed. "Where did you come from?"

"I don't know," the coyote replied, "but here I am. Who are you?"

"They call me Old Man Coyote. You are a coyote too; you are my true brother. Come, let me show you around."

The two coyotes traveled together across the earth until the newcomer asked Old Man Coyote, "Are there creatures other than the ones you have shown me? Why don't you make something new?"

"I will," Coyote answered.

The professor listened intently as Yellow Brow continued describing the many twists and turns of the Crow story of how the earth and all its creatures came to be.

The records Robert Lowie made of Yellow Brow's version of creation tell us a great deal about the Crow Indians

A drawing by George Catlin of a Crow warrior. Catlin later wrote, "No part of the human race could present a more picturesque and thrilling appearance on horseback than a party of Crows rigged out in all their plumes and trappings."

and their view of the world. Although most modern Crow attend Christian churches and *all* are Americans, they are nevertheless part of a distinct tradition that does not share many of the values that Americans of European descent hold most sacred. Ever since the early 19th century, when the tribe first encountered non-Indians, Crow Indians have often rejected the beliefs of white society simply because they are so different from their own.

Most Americans, for instance, place a high value on the individual. This idea is reflected in the Christian belief that people should have a personal relationship with God and in the philosophy of democracy. Individualism originated among white Americans' European ancestors in part because of the Bible's creation story, which asserts that God made man in his own image. As Yellow Brow's story shows, the Crow did not traditionally share this view. Although the Crow valued people's individual strengths, they believed humans to be equals of animals and plants in their Creator's eye. For them, people were not created in the image of God; they were made at the same time as the other creatures with whom they would share the earth as partners.

The biblical concept of the Creator is also very different from the Crow's. In the Bible, God alone makes the world in six days. In Yellow Brow's tale, creation is not a solitary, heroic act, but instead emerges from the conversation of three familiar animals with human emotions. Old Man Coyote is not an all-powerful force like the Christian and Jewish God. "God's power" merely expresses itself through his and the other animals' actions.

Also unlike the biblical creation, Yellow Brow's story has no moral. In the Judeo-Christian tradition, God's earth is His domain. People, therefore, owe the Creator respect and are expected to obey rules of behavior that are handed down by God. Although the Crow had rules of right and wrong, they did not traditionally look to their Creator as the author of a moral code. The Crow's creation story neither mentions any commandments from God nor condemns any actions as sins. Men and women appear in the middle of the creation process and, unlike Adam and Eve, are given no special role to play as lords of the earth. Their creation is simply a fact.

Jews and Christians begin their creation story with God separating the darkness from the light; the Crow begin theirs with Old Man Coyote gazing across the sea, which exists before the earth was made. This illustrates another difference between the two traditions: their sense of time. In the Judeo-Christian view, time began at the moment of creation. History ever since is seen as a process of moving forward and upward, which Europeans and Americans consider "progress." In the Crow's tradition, creation was gradual, and time was measured by seasons rather than years. For them, time did not march upward to the tune of "progress," but

A view of the Bighorn Canyon in the center of the beautiful Crow homeland.

instead evolved slowly in no fixed pattern.

This concept of progress has long clouded the image of American Indians in the eyes of non-Indians. When many Americans today think of Indians, they envision a man wearing a feather war bonnet mounted on a horse. Although awesome and powerful, this warrior seems to be a member of a "backward" or "primitive" people who lived only in the past until they surrendered to the "progress" of Western civilization.

Many of the Crow Indians in the late 18th and early 19th centuries were in fact superb warriors and buffalo hunters who often wore magnificent costumes fashioned from skin and bone. Called Beaux Hommes (Handsome Men) by early French explorers, they inhabited a lush land teeming with game. They rode swift ponies, lived in tipis, and honored their war heroes with great feather bonnets whose tails dragged along the ground.

But the mounted Crow warriors' time on history's stage was quite brief. The horse and buffalo were central to their culture for only about 100 years. To represent these people with this single image, therefore, is foolish. This simplistic view also prevents us from appreciating the Crow's special values and beliefs. Without an understanding of these, we cannot comprehend what bound them together in the past and what binds them together today.

The Crow and their ancestors have inhabited the Plains of central North America in present-day Montana for hundreds of years. It is a vivid world of grassy prairies, rivers, wildlife, and mountain forests. Throughout their history they have believed themselves lucky to live in so beautiful a homeland. Old Man Coyote, the ducks, and the power they brought to the earth have showered many blessings on the Crow. Old Man Coyote said it best and most simply: It is good. ▲

Paris-ka-too-pa (Two Crows), in an 1832 painting by George Catlin.

TRIBAL
ORIGINS

Eelapuash, a great Crow leader during the first quarter of the 19th century, once said that the tribe's homeland was "a good country because the Great Spirit put it in exactly the right place." Eelapuash's statement captures the two-part process by which the Crow believe their tribe came to inhabit the beautiful country near the Bighorn Mountains. First, the Creator made and placed the Crow homeland on the earth; then, the Crow found it because it was "in exactly the right place."

The Crow tribe was formed over a 300-year period that began about the time English settlers first landed in North America and ended in the early 19th century when the Crow first encountered the descendants of these newcomers. There are two sources of information about this process: archaeological findings and the teachings of tribal elders. Archaeologists learn about ancient peoples from what they call material culture. This includes the many things a community leaves behind, such as handmade items made by individuals—tools, weapons, and art objects—as well as building foundations, human remains, and even garbage. In contrast, the Crow collect information about their past from the stories that have been passed from generation to generation for hundreds of years. Only in the 20th century have the Crow transferred this oral testimony to written form. Although sometimes these sources provide conflicting information, both scholars and Crow teachers agree on the basic outlines of the tribe's early history.

Like other Indians—and most other people in the world—the Crow's ancestors spent much of the past 12,000 years hunting animals for meat and gathering edible seeds and berries. In North America, the end of the last Ice Age caused the glaciers that had covered the continent to draw northward. In their wake, both game and plant life multi-

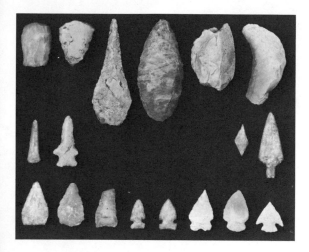

These stone spear points and arrowheads were excavated from the Crow homeland in 1942. Such artifacts help archaeologists build a picture of the past.

plied. The human population also grew and soon began to take advantage of the changing environment by moving north into territory that had previously lain beneath sheets of ice. People developed tools, such as the spear thrower and the bow and arrow, to improve their chances in the hunt. They also learned to make baskets for storing and transporting food and to domesticate dogs to help in their work.

The earliest peoples to inhabit the Great Plains traveled throughout the region in small bands, hunting game and gathering widely scattered wild plants for their food. Following herds of animals or seeking out areas with ripe vegetation, they moved from place to place with changes in the season and the availability of food sources.

The greatest event to occur on the Great Plains in the thousand years before Europeans landed in North America was the introduction of a hardy variety of corn called northern flint to the Missouri and Mississippi river valleys in about A.D. 400. People in this region had farmed corn since the 1st century A.D., but northern flint yielded a much more reliable harvest than the types of corn grown previously. These farmers could now produce large enough crops and could rely less on hunting and gathering for their food.

Indian farmers' harvests of northern flint were often so large that they could store some of their crop for future use. These surpluses increased when Indians learned to plant two crops a year— one in the early spring and one in the summer. They then began to trade their surplus crops to neighboring tribes in exchange for animal hides or other objects. Thus, while the people of Europe were establishing trade networks among market towns during the Middle Ages, the people of North America were also developing regional economies. Plains people soon developed trade networks, through which goods were carried long distances. Indians in the Great Lakes region could obtain Rocky Mountain obsidian (a hard stone excellent for making knife blades); groups along the Atlantic coast and Mississippi River valley could get copper from peoples in what is now Michigan; and the inhabitants of the Missouri River could trade for shells from the Gulf of Mexico.

As the peoples of the Great Plains learned the techniques of agriculture, they began to seek areas with fertile land and good sources of water in which to establish communities. One group of farmers gradually migrated up to what is now the Missouri River valley, while another traveled from Lakes Michigan and Superior to the Red, Assiniboine, Saskatchewan, and James rivers. By about the year 1000, members of both groups were living along the banks of the Missouri River in present-day North Dakota. These communities of farmers contained some of the ancestors of the modern Crow.

The farmers along the Missouri River settled into villages where they lived for at least part of the year. The people in these villages had similar beliefs and spoke related languages. However, these groups were not tribes because they did not have a strong sense of group identity.

Village homes were earth lodges—spacious, dome-shaped dwellings made of wood, grass, and earth. Each

A Hidatsa village of earth lodges along the Knife River, drawn by George Catlin in 1832.

earth lodge housed several families. As more and more people began living together in close quarters, the need for rules and regulations to govern the inhabitants of each village grew. The earth lodge settlements developed a system of divided leadership. Religious leaders controlled ceremonies; the elders of groups of families known as clans made political decisions; and elderly women, who usually owned the garden plots, supervised the farming.

Although the early villagers had been attracted to the Plains by the rich farmland along the upper Missouri River, they soon became aware of the game in the region and began to hunt the buffalo that roamed the grasslands for food and for hides. Groups of hunters stalked individual animals and killed them with carefully aimed arrows shot from bows. These people also organized communal hunts, when they would kill a large number of buffalo by driving an entire herd over a cliff or into an enclosure, where they could easily slaughter the trapped animals. Luckily for the Missouri River farmers, most buffalo have poor vision and little intelligence, so these methods served them fairly well; they could be confident that their corn soup would be filled with hunks of buffalo meat during the long, bleak winter. But buffalo hunts were not always successful, and farming corn still offered most village people their greatest security and most reliable source of food.

Some farmers, however, preferred the hunt. During the 1500s, or perhaps earlier, small groups of farmers from the Missouri River region began to spend the winter hunting on the Plains. They became expert trackers and learned to stalk elk, antelope, and other game, as well as buffalo.

The Crow trace their ancestry to one of these small groups. The hunters were Awatixa, one of three divisions of the Hidatsa Indians whose ancestors had centuries before migrated westward, possibly from what is now Minnesota. Beginning in about 1100, the Awatixa settled along the Knife River, a small tributary that flows into the Missouri some 50 miles upriver from present-day Bismarck, North Dakota. From this location, they traveled on the Plains to hunt and explore. By the end of the 16th century, bands of Awatixa hunters started to spend more and more time west of the Missouri. Eventually some abandoned their villages to hunt on the Plains year-round.

On a high bluff overlooking the junction of the Yellowstone and Missouri rivers is a site that provides clues to how the Crow's ancestors adapted to life on the Plains. In the 1930s, archaeologists came to this spot (near present-day Glendive, Montana) to investigate what seemed to be the remains of an ancient village located on a ranch owned by a man named Thomas Hagen. They were not disappointed. At first the village at the Hagen Site appeared similar to settlements to the east of the Knife River that had been previously excavated. Like them, it had been built on high land and com-

An early-19th-century engraving after a painting of the junction of the Yellowstone and Missouri rivers by Karl Bodmer. This area is near the Hagen site, where archaeologists excavated a village that may have been inhabited by the Mountain Crows' ancestors.

manded a sweeping view of a river and the surrounding countryside. But the Hagen site was different: Instead of containing a cluster of earth lodges, it had only one. Most of its inhabitants seemed to have lived in temporary shelters—probably early versions of the conical tipis that housed the later Plains Indians. Although archaeologists discovered a number of agricultural tools, such as digging sticks and hoes made from the shoulder blades of buffalo, they found too few to conclude that the village's inhabitants had relied on farming for their livelihood. However, the bones of deer and buffalo littered the Hagen site.

Scholars are still not sure exactly who lived in the village near Glendive or exactly how old the settlement is. (Their best estimate is that it was inhabited by the end of the 1600s.) But archaeologists are certain that the Hagen Site represents a transition from the settled farming routine of the Missouri River Hidatsa to the hunting life later enjoyed by the Crow. The village might have been the home of one of the first bands of Awatixa Hidatsa to migrate west toward the Bighorn Mountains, or it could have been an experimental settlement established by Hidatsa who had left their villages in search of new land to farm.

Over time those Awatixa Hidatsa who were most inclined to hunt moved further and further west. The longer they were separated from their kin and the farming life, the fewer reasons they had to return to the Missouri River region. Eventually the Awatixa began to live permanently in the valley of the Yellowstone River and along its tributaries. There they came to think of themselves not as Hidatsa, but part of a separate people—the tribe that would later be called the Crow.

There is no written record of the process by which these early Hidatsa hunters became Crow, but there are many

Crow men hunting buffalo, painted by Karl Bodmer in the 1830s. On horseback, early Crow hunters could easily travel across the Plains in search of wild game.

accounts of the tribe's origin in its oral history. Elder Crow tell of the Awatixa's migration from the east and of the years they spent looking for the "right place" to settle. For example, Joe Medicine Crow, one of the tribe's modern historians, says that the Crow's Awatixa ancestors first came to the Plains in about 1600 and that their migration from the Missouri River to the Bighorn Mountains took about a century. According to Medicine Crow, the group first headed northwest toward what is now Canada and settled for a time in modern Alberta:

> The people of this new tribe, still without a name, referred to themselves as "Our Side." One day, the leaders called a council. The consensus of opinion was, "The place is too harsh; the winters are long and cold. We must move and find a better place to live." Once again, they packed their dogs and wolves and headed south through the valleys and passes of the mountains.

In this and other versions of the story, the migrants traveled first south to what is now the Great Salt Lake in northern Utah, then east to Oklahoma, and finally northwest up the Missouri River and across Nebraska to Wyoming.

While this group was in the process of migrating, a new trade item was being introduced to the native peoples of North America. In 1598, Spanish settlers arrived in what is now the southwestern United States, determined to establish a new province for the Spanish empire. They brought with them ponies from Europe. The Indians had never seen these strong, swift, intelligent animals. But soon the effects of the introduction of these creatures would roar across the West like a herd of frightened buffalo and change the life of all Indians of the Plains.

Initially the Spaniards were determined to keep their horses out of the hands of Indians. Members of southwestern tribes were able to acquire a small number from the Spanish invaders, but Indian people did not obtain entire herds of horses until 1680. In that year, the Pueblo tribes of the Rio Grande valley rose up in revolt against the Spaniards and chased them out of the region. These tribes then began to breed the ponies that the Spaniards had left behind and to trade those they did not need themselves to Indians to the north and east. By 1700 the Spanish had reestablished their control over the Southwest, but by then the Shoshone Indians had a large number of horses. The Shoshone in turn began to trade their surplus to Indian groups who lived to their north in the region of the Yellowstone and Bighorn rivers.

Mounted on these ponies, the descendants of the early Awatixa pioneers had no fear of starvation during the hunt. On horseback, they could travel long distances faster and more easily than ever before. New vistas of exploration and adventure opened before them. They ranged south into present-day Wyoming, west to the Rockies, north to the headwaters of the Missouri River, and east to visit their friends and kin along the Knife River. By 1750 this group had established itself as the Mountain Crow, one of the two great divisions of the modern tribe.

As the Mountain Crow were traveling through the Plains, a second Hidatsa migration was under way. Starting in about 1700, a century after the Mountain Crow's ancestors had left the Missouri Valley, another group abandoned the Hidatsa villages located near what is now Devil's Lake in eastern North Dakota. These Hidatsa were hunters who traveled regularly to the Plains to pursue the buffalo and other game abundant there.

Again, the Crow's oral testimony provides details of this migration that concur with archaeologists' hunches about when and how it occurred. There are many versions of this story, but most Crow narrators include two common elements. First, they tell of a leader named No Vitals who is given some tobacco seeds by the Creator, who explains that they represent the special identity of his people. In one version of the story, the Creator says to No Vitals, "The people I am making shall live all over the Earth, but those to whom I give this plant shall be few, and it shall make their hearts strong." In another version, the tobacco seeds come from a star: "On the side of the mountain a star was shining. [No Vitals] took it and brought it home, wrapped it up and showed it to no one. . . . He planted it . . . it grew.

He harvested it. . . . 'Thus we shall be people,' he said."

Second, all variations of the second migration story include an incident at a Hidatsa village. A buffalo wanders into a camp and is killed by the Hidatsa. They then refuse to share the buffalo meat with one group of villagers. In one version, a young man in this excluded group says to his leader, "I do not like these people. Let us move camp without them. We will go upstream and get to the mountains." In all versions, the group decides to move immediately. These people then pack their belongings and abandon their earth lodge villages for life on the Plains.

This group of migrants became the River Crow. They tended to hunt along the upper reaches of the Missouri River, although they frequently visited the Mountain Crow at their Yellowstone and Bighorn river homes. The River Crow probably received their first horses from the Mountain Crow. The latter lived closer to Indian traders in present-day New Mexico, the Crow's primary source of ponies.

The acquisition of horses undoubtedly accelerated the River Crow's devotion to hunting and travel. The two parts of the tribe maintained contact with one another, but because the River Crow had separated from the Hidatsa more recently than the Mountain Crow, they probably returned more often to the Missouri River villages than their kin did. Nevertheless, the two groups spoke the same language, shared sim-

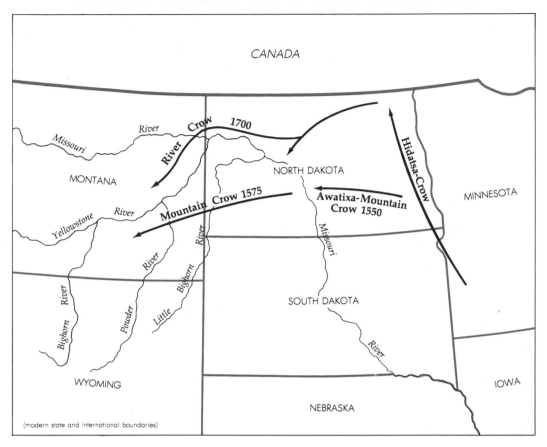

ilar stories of Old Man Coyote, and intermarried. These ties and their need to ally with one another against common enemies drew them together.

By 1750, with both groups' separation from the Hidatsa complete, the Crow Indians had come into existence as a distinct people. Members of the tribe called themselves the "Absaroka." In their language, this word referred to a large bird, which early French explorers believed was a Crow. The exact identity of the absaroka is now lost, but today tribal members still continue to refer to themselves as the "children of the long-beaked bird."

The development of the Crow's tribal identity had been a long, gradual process spurred by several factors. Some people had wanted to separate themselves from the Hidatsa primarily for religious reasons. The Hidatsa's beliefs allowed this to happen. The tribe did not have powerful religious leaders, and individuals who felt they were specially called upon by the Creator some-

A hide decorated by a Crow artist in the early 19th century with a narrative painting of warriors in battle.

times developed variations on tribal rituals. Over time, these rituals may have encouraged groups to leave their villages to form new divisions of the tribe. Others were probably prompted to leave the Hidatsa by the prospect of good hunting. Particularly after the introduction of horses, it was possible for a band to venture out onto the Plains and survive without the assistance of a permanent base camp. Still others might have decided to move away from the Hidatsa villages merely because they became tired of the humdrum routines required by the farmer's life.

Despite these different motivations, the people who opted for life on the Plains year-round came to share many things. They trusted in the lesson of their origin stories, that the Creator had selected them to be the inhabitants of a special place. They believed the tale about the coming of the tobacco plant and that caring for that plant was important to their survival. And they associated the excitement and freedom of the hunt with their people. To be a member of the Crow tribe, therefore, was to inhabit the Plains, to hunt, to revere tobacco, and to share a faith in the wisdom of No Vitals and the chiefs who followed him.

But being a Crow was not just a matter of belief. During the second half of the 1700s, the tribe established itself as a significant force on the Plains. In that period, the River and Mountain Crow cooperated to defend their homeland against Shoshone raiders from the south, Blackfoot enemies to the north and west, and Sioux buffalo hunters from the east. As inhabitants of the rich hunting territory positioned between trade routes that ran north from Mexico and south from Hudson Bay, the Crow were envied by many other Plains peoples. They grew rich exchanging hides and beautifully crafted clothing for ponies, guns, and tools. Crow traders sometimes journeyed as far east as the Missouri River and as far west as the plateau country of what are now Idaho and Oregon.

As the Crow worked and traveled together, they developed a distinct way of life that set them apart more sharply from other groups—both Indian and non-Indian. Unlike tribes of Indian farmers or the inhabitants of European communities, the Crow maintained all of their important institutions in mobile form. Their places of instruction were not schoolhouses but tipis; they did not find God in a building but in a sacred place or in a special object that they could carry from camp to camp. What it meant to be a member of the tribe could not be discovered in a permanent settlement, but only in the hearts and minds of the Crow people. ▲

Oo-je-en-a-he-ha (Woman Who Lives in a Bear's Den), painted by George Catlin in 1832.

THE CHILDREN
OF THE
LONG-BEAKED BIRD

On June 25, 1805, at about one o'clock in the afternoon, the Crow Indians paraded into written history. On that date, 645 brightly painted Crow men and women wearing their finest buckskin clothing and mounted on decorated ponies filed solemnly through the Hidatsa villages on the banks of the Missouri River. A witness to the scene was a young French-Canadian adventurer named François Antoine Larocque. He had come to the northern Plains to trade with the Indians there for beaver and otter pelts, which could be sold for high prices in eastern North American and European markets. During his travels, Larocque kept a detailed journal, in which appeared his description of this procession, the first eyewitness account of the Crow ever recorded.

The Crow's 1805 visit to their Hidatsa kin touched off days of feasting and trading. Amid this activity, La-rocque held a council with the tribe's leaders and won permission to accompany the Crow back to their homeland. Larocque's account of the summer he subsequently spent with the tribe was just one of several records made by non-Indian explorers who visited the Crow in the early 19th century. Although all of these journals contain errors and gaps, they offer unique snapshots of the confident Crow people on the eve of their first sustained contact with non-Indians. Information about the Crow's traditional customs and beliefs has also been compiled in the 20th century by anthropologists who have visited the tribe and interviewed elderly Crow about their past. The records of both early-19th-century adventurers and 20th-century anthropologists have created a large body of information that provides the basis of our picture of the Crow way of life more than 150 years ago.

At the outset of Larocque's account of his time among the Crow, he presented a description of the country where the tribe had migrated over the previous 500 years: "This nation inhabits the eastern part of the Rocky Mountains at the head of the River aux Roches Jaunes [literally, the river of yellow stones] . . . and close to the head of the Missouri." By this time, the Mountain Crow had settled in the Bighorn and Absaroka mountains. For most of the year they hunted on the plains south of the Yellowstone River, but they spent the winter in protected areas south of the modern Montana-Wyoming border. The River Crow ranged along the upper reaches of the Missouri River. They continued to pay frequent visits to their old relatives in the Hidatsa villages and often came in contact with the Assiniboine and Blackfoot Indians living to the north.

According to Larocque, there were "three principal tribes" of Crow. The Crow were actually still a single tribe; Larocque was noting their division into the River Crow and two smaller groups that had formed within the Mountain Crow: the "Main Body" and the "Kicked in the Bellies." The Main Body tended to travel west toward the Bighorn Mountains. The Kicked in the Bellies spent most of their time in the Little Bighorn and Powder River valleys in the eastern portion of Crow territory.

Although the tribe was divided into these separate units, the Crow frequently visited back and forth between camps. Larocque reported that he had "never seen them remain any time in their tents alone. . . . They are social, are fond of company and are lonesome when alone." But visiting relatives also served a practical purpose. The Crow needed to band together in order to guard their homeland from invasion by enemy tribes who wanted to hunt the plentiful game in Crow country. The Blackfoot to the north, the Shoshone to the south, and the Sioux and Cheyenne to the southeast were constant menaces. To protect their lands, the Crow sought friends in neighboring tribes as well. The Hidatsa were the Crow's most dependable allies, but Larocque noted that the Crow also had a steady trading relationship with the Shoshone, from whom they obtained horses and Spanish glass beads. The Crow also traded with the Flathead, who brought horses and a sprinkling of handicrafts—blankets and food containers—with them when they left their plateau homeland and crossed the Rockies to hunt each summer. By visiting with these trusted trading partners and their kin, the Crow were able to maintain their strength and unity despite the threat of attack from rival tribes.

In Larocque's description of Crow country, he reported that the tribe's territory "abounds so much in buffalo and deer . . . [that] they find no difficulty in finding provision for a numerous family." The fur trader noted correctly that the Crow had large households and that many men had more than one wife. But Larocque did not stay in Crow country long enough to learn how the

A Crow mother and her child, photographed by Edward S. Curtis in 1908.

tribe organized its families. Like many other non-Indian visitors who followed him, Larocque saw the tribe as simply a collection of friends and relatives who traveled wherever they pleased. Although to these strangers the Crow appeared to live in perfect freedom, they in fact ordered their society according to strict rules.

One of the first people to gain some understanding of how the tribe was organized was Thomas LeForge, an 18-year-old white American who set off in 1868 to travel through the Bighorn Mountains in search of game and adventure. Before long, LeForge fell in with a band of Crow Indians who were

hunting there. They took him to their camp, where he lived in the tipi of Yellow Leggings, the leader of the band. LeForge and Yellow Leggings's son, Three Irons, quickly became good friends. After several weeks, Yellow Leggings called his followers together and announced that he was going to adopt Thomas LeForge. "This young man is going to be my son," the old man said. "Thus," LeForge later recalled, "I became a Crow Indian."

Whereas Americans and Europeans tend to define who they are by their race or occupation, Crow traditionally identify themselves by referring to their family. The Crow were bound together by kinship rather than by a uniform set of beliefs or written laws; the tribe was essentially a group of many interrelated families. Therefore, by adopting LeForge into his family, Yellow Leggings granted him the equivalent of citizenship in the tribe.

Young LeForge loved his life as a Crow. He hunted, trapped, and explored the Absaroka and Bighorn mountains with other young tribesmen. It took LeForge two years to master the Crow language, but he reported that when he had, he was "on good terms" with everyone in the band.

Soon after, LeForge—then a handsome 20-year-old sporting a mustache and dressed in moccasins and buckskin—took notice of an 18-year-old Crow woman, whom he called Cherry. Following Crow custom, he paid a visit to Cherry's mother and brother and told them he wanted to marry her.

(continued on page 38)

CROW KINSHIP TERMINOLOGY

In 1868, Thomas LeForge, a white adventurer, was adopted into the Crow tribe. In his memoirs, LeForge later wrote that initially one of the most difficult things for him to understand about his new society was the way members of Crow families referred to one another. For instance, a Crow woman would call her mother's sister by the Crow word for *mother*. Although confusing to outsiders, this terminology made perfect sense to the Crow. Like the members of every society, they had their own system of terms to denote kinship, and like every such system, it was an expression of the interactions among the people who used it.

These two kinship charts illustrate the differences between the kinship terminology traditionally used by the Crow and that used by non-Indian Americans and Europeans today. Both charts include three generations of the family of Cherry, the Crow woman who married Thomas LeForge. (According to LeForge, Cherry had a mother, a father, and three brothers— two adopted and one biological. For the sake of illustration, she is shown as having two sets of grandparents, aunts, uncles, and cousins.) The label beneath each symbol representing a family member gives the name Cherry would call that relative according to the system represented by the chart.

The importance of clan affiliation in Crow society accounts for many of the differences in the two charts. Crow clan membership was matrilineal, or traced through one's mother's side. Cherry referred to her male cousins on her mother's side, who belonged to Cherry's clan, by the same term she used for her three brothers. Similarly, she referred to her female relatives who belonged to her clan (her mother's sisters or her mother's sister's daughters) as sisters. Unlike many Indian tribes, Crow individuals felt a special bond for close blood relatives who were not members of their own clan. For instance, Cherry called her paternal aunt *mother* and her paternal uncle *father* even though they belonged to her father's clan and she belonged to her mother's.

This representation of Crow kinship relations is greatly simplified. Crow Indians considered many other people—such as members of clans allied to their own—family members. They also had many more terms in their language than there are in English to denote relatives. (For example, girls used a different word for *father* than boys did.) These complexities, as LeForge and the non-Indian visitors who followed him discovered, are indicative of the tremendous importance of family relationships in Crow life.

TWO VIEWS OF CHERRY'S FAMILY

Symbols: ● female   = marriage | descent

▲ male   — siblings

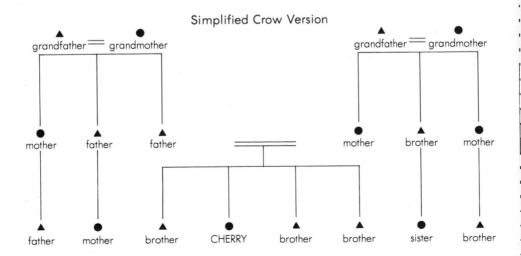

American/European Version

Simplified Crow Version

(continued from page 35)

(Usually a Crow male would approach the bride-to-be's parents, but Cherry's father had been killed in battle.) After they agreed, a wedding, which consisted of a gift-giving ceremony, was arranged. "I gave presents [including blankets, horses, and tools] to her full brother and two adopted brothers," LeForge wrote, "and they in turn gave presents to me." Cherry also received gifts from her relatives and friends. Cherry then moved her and LeForge's belongings into a new home where the couple and Cherry's mother would live.

LeForge learned that Cherry's "people were of the burnt (or sore lips) clan." As he and later visitors came to understand, a clan was the Crow's basic unit of social organization. Each clan was composed of a group of related families and therefore included many more people than a nuclear family (parents and their children), the basic social unit in the United States today. The Crow word for clan, *ashmmaleaxia*, was often translated as "driftwood lodges." Just as pieces of driftwood became lodged together as they were swept

Three Crow couples dancing, drawn on paper from a ledger book by Crow leader and artist Deaf Bull in 1881.

down the Yellowstone River each spring, members of a clan were joined together as a single unit.

Not all members of a clan lived or traveled together, however. Clans included too many people for that to be possible. The Crow also did not want to have only one clan represented in a band of travelers because clan members were considered so closely related that people within the same clan could not marry. Therefore, members of several clans traveled together so that no one would have to seek a mate from outside the camp. A person's clan affiliation, however, was still very important. Members of the same clan were more likely to assist one another at special religious ceremonies, to hunt together, and to share pride in each other's good fortune in battle.

The Crow observed a strict code of behavior based on their relation to one another. Youngsters, for instance, were expected to pay respect to male elders within their clan (known as clan uncles) and to their father's kin, whom they often called "mother" or "father." Adults would also honor these relatives by addressing them with special dignity and by giving them a portion of their kill from hunting expeditions.

Other relationships called for different behavior. The Crow believed that some relatives had to be avoided. Married men and women, for example, were not permitted to speak with their parents-in-law. Some relatives had to be teased. Children of men who belonged to the same clan were called "joking cousins"; they were expected to keep each other in line through constant ribbing and joke playing. Such roles were important in Crow society because cooperation among tribespeople was essential for their survival as they traveled from camp to camp. Discipline in the form of jokes and teasing was therefore much more effective than harsh punishments.

Thomas LeForge learned that to the Crow a family included many people— blood relatives, fellow clan members, and members of the clan of one's father. Sometimes this expanded definition of family was puzzling. As LeForge wrote, "The number of genuine offspring children in any family was not easily discoverable. If one said, 'This is my son,' . . . the statement was never questioned. If any couple had several children when they apparently should have had but one . . . it was not polite to make references to the situation. The fact that a woman carried on her back a baby was not proof that it was her own." But even though these customs were confusing to outsiders, they were of great practical value to the Crow. Even though the people of the tribe were divided into hunting bands that were dispersed throughout the Yellowstone and Missouri river valleys, all Crow felt special ties to the members of other bands. Whenever a group of Crow met another on the prairie or along a mountain stream, each person could be sure that among the strangers would be a relative. These ties bonded the tribespeople together and gave them strength against their common enemies.

In the early 1800s, bands of Crow traveled in an annual cycle. Their schedule and route were determined by the availability of game and wild roots and berries. In the spring, when chokecherries bloomed, they would begin to gather different types of wild plants, including wild turnip, rhubarb, and strawberries. In the summer, they would collect ripened chokecherries and plums. At that time, bands would also come together to conduct religious ceremonies and group buffalo hunts. Throughout the year, individuals and small parties of Crow would hunt rabbits, deer, elk, and other game. As fall approached, the bands would separate into smaller groups that would seek refuge from the winter weather in the protected mountain valleys of the Rockies or along the bottomlands of the upper Missouri River.

Interaction with other tribes—both friends and enemies—also motivated the movement of bands of Crow across the length and breadth of their territory. Bands would sometimes travel to escape raids staged by the Blackfoot and the Sioux or to launch revenge attacks on these tribes. They also often set out for the Missouri River or the western slope of the Rockies to trade with their Indian allies there.

Temporary non-Indian visitors often reported that these bands simply wandered across the Plains in search of food and the excitement of battle. But those who spent time with the Crow knew better. Larocque, for example, wrote that a "band of young men" regulated camp life by dictating when people could hunt and when their group would move to a new site. These groups, known as warrior societies, also set the schedule of religious ceremonies. Larocque reported that those who disobeyed a warrior society's orders were "punished by a beating or [their weapons] were broken or their tents cut to pieces."

Membership in warrior societies was open to all young men who had distinguished themselves in battle. In the 1800s, the Foxes and the Lumpwood were the most prominent societies; others—the Big Dogs, the Muddy Hands, and the Ravens—were of less importance. Each society recruited promising young men, chose its own leaders, and established customs and emblems to represent it, much as different branches of the military services do today.

During the spring and summer, the warrior societies competed with each other for prestige and honors. They hunted and raided together, flaunting their successes in public parades and teasing their rivals when they fell short of success. Sometimes members of one society would even capture and marry the wives of those of another. Despite this rivalry, all disputes were forgotten when winter came. With the cold weather, warriors retreated to their earth lodges to tell stories of their exploits and prepare their weapons and finery for the coming year.

A 1913 photograph of two Crow women picking berries, one of the many wild plants the tribe gathered to supplement its diet of animal meat.

Warrior societies were led by chiefs who had attained this status by performing four types of military exploits: leading a war party, capturing an enemy's horse, being the first to touch an enemy in a battle, and snatching an enemy warrior's weapon. The men in each society who had accumulated the largest number of these war honors were regarded as the chiefs by general agreement of its members.

Each camp contained several other people who acted as leaders. Holy men and women who were believed to have special spiritual powers performed religious ceremonies. Others, whom non-Indians often called "medicine men," were knowledgeable about the medicinal properties of herbs and other means of curing illnesses. Elders in a particular clan or household usually took responsibility for settling family

A narrative painting on muslin of a Crow warrior fighting enemy Indians. The headdress on the Crow, who is pictured in various stages of the battle, identifies him as a member of the Lumpwood warrior society.

disputes or comforting people who had been wronged.

The affairs of entire bands were dictated by a combination of warrior society chiefs and elders. These leaders met together to plan their band's movements and to regulate the assignment of duties. Non-Indian explorers and soldiers usually referred to the people who made these decisions as chiefs.

"Chief," of course, is an English word; the best equivalent in the Crow language is *bacheeitche*, which means "good man." The difference between these two terms is revealing. Unlike European kings or American presidents, Crow leaders of the early 19th century did not have their power spelled out in documents; instead it was granted to them by the tribe according to their ability to live up to the Crow ideals of brav-

ery, generosity, and loyalty. When chiefs fell short of these ideals, they lost their power. Thus, in order to keep their position, Crow leaders had to stand out in their communities while continuing to participate in the daily life of their clan, band, or warrior society. They could never be too far removed from their followers.

The Crow's traditional form of government was well suited to a way of life based on hunting, family togetherness, and travel through a variety of environments. LeForge had a glimpse of this ancient political system during his years with the tribe. Later he reported that the Crow "had among themselves law and order more effectively prevalent than among any community of white people I have known. Their laws were few but they were well enforced."

The richness of the Crow's religious life was more difficult for visitors to appreciate. Larocque, for example, wrote, "I do not know what they believe . . . more than that they believe in good and bad spirits and in a Supreme master of life." The Crow were in fact a deeply religious people, but because they had no permanent churches it was hard for newcomers to understand their beliefs. For the Crow, religion was not reserved for Sunday; it was a part of everyday life. They believed that they had been blessed both by the creation of the earth and by their placement on the beautiful northern Plains; therefore, the Creator was never far from their mind.

The Crow regarded their homeland as proof of the Creator's presence. Because the Creator was nearby, he could be contacted through special ceremonies. The most common of these was the vision quest. In this ritual, a young man would leave his home for several days and retreat to an isolated area. There alone, he would fast and pray to the Creator to give him guidance in the form of a vivid dream. Sometimes, in order to help bring on these visions, the boy would cut himself and offer a gift of his own flesh to the Creator. When a vision quest was successful, a spirit would appear and instruct the boy how to behave or warn him against certain actions. Often this spirit would take the form of an animal, especially a bear or a buffalo. After the quest, this animal would become the boy's guardian.

To express gratitude for the Creator's blessings or to seek guidance for the future, groups of Crow gathered to perform tribal rituals. The most important of these were the Sun Dance and the tobacco planting. Sun Dances were held in the summer to help warriors avenge the killing of a relative or close friend in battle. Assisted and guided by a holy man, a warrior who was seeking revenge pledged to carry out the dance. An elder (called his Sun Dance father) organized the necessary dancers and costumes and oversaw the erection of a special earth lodge, in which the ritual was to be performed. Drummers, singers, fellow warriors, and relatives then spent several days preparing for the dance by making special moccasins, gathering buffalo tongues to feed the participants, and preparing the pledger for his ordeal. The last task required prayers to the Sun Dance father's doll, an object that the Crow believed carried great spiritual power. Sun Dance dolls were usually made according to instructions that were received from the Creator in visions. They were carefully protected and passed down from one generation to another.

When the ceremony finally began, the young warrior emerged from his tipi and moved solemnly between two lines of people that marked a path to the Sun Dance lodge. When the pledger arrived at the lodge, an elaborate dance began. Urged on by their families and friends, the Sun Dance father, fellow warriors, and the pledger moved to the rhythm of the onlookers' songs and the beat of drums. Most of the dancers stopped from time to time, but the pledger, blowing an eagle-bone whistle in time with the drumbeats, danced continuously. The Sun Dance father's doll was suspended before him throughout the dancing. The warrior continued to dance and stare at the doll until he fell into a trance. In this state, he received a vision that convinced him that he would be successful in punishing his enemies for the death of his friend or relative. The vision also inspired others to join him on the raid.

The tobacco planting was a commemoration of No Vitals's encounter with the Creator at the time of the River Crow's separation from the Hidatsa.

A female leader of the Tobacco Society, photographed by Robert Lowie during an adoption ceremony in 1910.

According to the Crow's oral tradition, the Creator gave the leader tobacco seeds as a special gift to the Crow and told No Vitals that they should be planted each year. The planting was supervised by the Tobacco Society, an organization of men and women from all the bands of the tribe. Within the Tobacco Society were several different chapters, each of which adopted new members (usually couples) annually and met regularly in the fall and winter for dances. In the spring, the society planted a special ceremonial variety of tobacco gardens in special places. In the fall, its members harvested the tobacco seeds and stored them until they could be planted the following year. (Although the Crow smoked tobacco that they obtained through trade with other Indians, they never used the sacred variety.) The Tobacco Society's activities reminded all Crow of their obligation to the Creator and of their ties to each other as members of the tribe that he honored with the gift of these plants.

Although the Sun Dance and the tobacco planting were the most important religious rituals to the tribe, their observance took only a fraction of the time the Crow devoted to religious activities. Crow people sought visions wherever they traveled. For instance, men and women often lay in tobacco fields in hopes of receiving a message from a spirit. Also, the Crow always carried "medicines"—objects that they believed contained power granted by the Creator—from camp to camp. These medicines ranged widely in size and power. Some were small articles, such as a part of an animal, that recalled a guardian who had appeared in a vision. Others were large bundles containing a variety of sacred objects. The most important of these items were sacred rocks, which were thought to have special power and to require special care.

The people who Larocque believed followed no organized religion also performed a variety of lesser rituals and ceremonies. These included the Bear Song Dance, the Sacred Pipe Dance, and feasts held to celebrate major events, such as victories in raiding or war. Each required that friends and family members cooperate and follow the orders of their leaders in order to make all the necessary preparations. All of these rituals reflected the tribe's reverence for the Creator and its members' belief that his power could appear in almost any form at almost any time.

Just as the Crow had a rich religious life without attending church, their children learned everything they needed to know to perform the roles they would play as adults without ever spending a day in a classroom. Each of the groups in Crow society—clans, warrior societies, religious organizations, and families—helped to teach children how to participate in social and religious activities. Youngsters were instructed in proper behavior by being encouraged to observe and imitate their clan elders. Warrior societies offered children advanced training in tracking animals and scouting enemies. Religious groups, such as the Tobacco Society, taught

their young members the elements of Crow beliefs and the meaning of their rituals. Therefore, although the Crow had no schools, children had every adult in the tribe as a teacher.

Families gave young Crow an education in everyday matters. Children especially looked to their "fathers" and "mothers" (their mother's siblings as well as their natural parents) and to their grandparents for instruction. Sometimes children would become attached to childless couples who might adopt them and take them into their lodge. When this happened, the children's new parents (and clan relations)

A 1908 photograph of a Crow woman cleaning a buffalo hide by scraping it with a piece of bone.

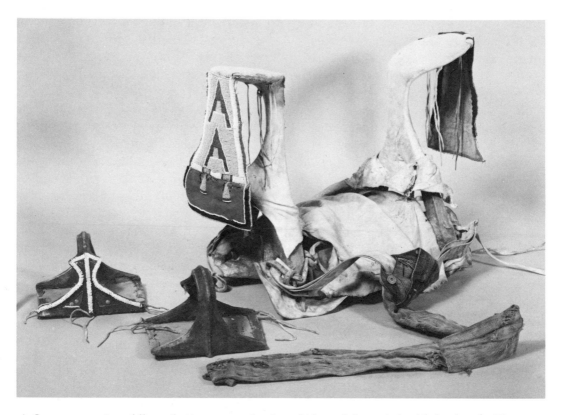

A Crow woman's saddle and stirrups, made of rawhide and decorated with beadwork. Women who were skilled on horseback could ride with the tribe's warriors.

would take on the responsibility for their education and their biological mother and father would become less important in their life.

The Crow specified some tasks as women's work and some as men's work. The lessons children were taught, therefore, depended on their sex. Girls were instructed in the female tasks of butchering buffalo killed in hunts and processing their hides. They also learned to sew this leather into moccasins and tipi covers and to make all the tools and clothing their families needed. Because women were the central figures in family and clan relationships, the home was their province. They owned and used tools, erected the tipis, and were the guardians of their husbands' shields. These activities placed them in charge of most day-to-day activities within a Crow camp.

Crow boys were taught how to track and hunt game. At an early age they were encouraged to hunt birds and rabbits; they often brought rabbit skins to girls to tan and cure. (Little girls sometimes used them or pieces of scrap buffalo hides to make miniature play tipis.) Boys were prepared to take over the male jobs of defending their camp, going on raids against their enemies, and, as members of the warrior societies, leading their band to new hunting or camping grounds.

Despite this division of labor, the Crow did not insist that *only* men do men's work and *only* women do women's work. The Crow accepted, even celebrated, people who were different from the group or who seemed specially suited to a particular activity. Thus, if a woman showed unusual skill on horseback, she might ride with the warriors. Similarly, if a man displayed an interest in household jobs, he was permitted to tan hides and make clothing. There was in fact a separate category of men, called *bate*, who preferred to dress and live as women. They were not only accepted but also revered by the Crow, who believed that the bate had a special tie to the Creator.

Despite its informal appearance, the traditional world of the Crow was regulated by family and clan ties; by political, religious, and war leaders; and by customs that all tribespeople respected and observed. The strangers who thought the tribe lived in complete freedom failed to appreciate the sense of group responsibility that all the Crow felt and that brought order to their seemingly unstructured way of life. ▲

Very Sweet Man *by George Catlin, painted in 1832.*

THE ARRIVAL
OF THE
WHITE MAN

The Crow knew of non-Indians (and probably saw them) long before whites began to visit their villages. But their daily life was not affected by these strangers until the first decade of the 19th century, when a steady stream of non-Indians started to arrive in Crow country. By 1825 many American fur traders were well established in the Yellowstone Valley. By 1850 canvas-covered wagons filled with non-Indian settlers bound for Oregon and California were a commonplace feature of the region's landscape. In a short period of time, the Crow were forced to adapt to the presence of an alien race in their homeland. They had to adjust as well to the ideas and demands of these newcomers, who would eventually seek to control much of the Crow's territory and who would quickly bring about drastic changes in their traditional way of life.

Like François Antoine Larocque, many of the earliest non-Indians to meet the Crow came to their lands because they wanted to trade with the tribe. For more than 200 years, non-Indian traders had been approaching groups of Indians with offers to exchange European or American manufactured goods for things the Indians had that non-Indians wanted to buy. Traders in the first colonies established by the English on the Atlantic Coast bargained for food, but elsewhere they looked to Indians as suppliers of rich beaver, fox, and otter furs. Indians of many tribes had centuries of experience in trapping these animals and cleaning their pelts, which they sewed into winter clothing. Fur hats and coats were also popular in Europe and the eastern United States at the time, so traders could easily sell the furs they obtained from the Indians for a handsome profit.

When Larocque first met the Crow chiefs in 1805, he encouraged their friendship by giving them the following presents: 4 axes, 8 ivory combs, 10 seashells, 8 steels and flints (implements for starting fires), smoking tobacco, beads, rooster feathers, 28 knives, red paint, 96 rings, 48 steel awls (tools for making holes in leather), several pieces of glass, 1,000 musket balls, and musket powder. With these gifts, Larocque hoped to impress the Crow with the types of goods he could offer them in exchange for beaver and otter skins. This list is like a catalog of the items later traders would bring to the Crow as the era of direct exchange between the tribe and outsiders opened.

Many of Larocque's presents were steel tools. The Crow had traditionally made awls, knives, and hatchets from stone or bone, but they soon came to prefer ones made from steel because they stayed sharper longer and were difficult to break. They discovered, too, that steel tools were easier to use. With a steel ax they could cut a tipi pole or chop firewood in a fraction of the time it took to do the work with a heavy stone hatchet. With steel awls Crow women could quickly pierce hides with holes through which they would string strips of leather or sinew to make tipi covers or clothes. They could also carve more delicate decorations on leather with these tools than they could with awls made of stone.

The Crow also desired trade goods that they could use to adorn themselves, their clothing, or other belong-

A rawhide container, or parfleche, made by a Crow in the 1840s. This parfleche was decorated by scraping away portions of the upper layer of hide with a steel awl to create an incised design.

ings. Warriors liked to place ivory combs in their long hair. Women sewed seashells onto dresses or ceremonial robes. Feathers were attached to war bonnets, and red paint was used to decorate people's face and body for special occasions. The Crow wore rings on their fingers or tied them to horse bridles as a flashy decoration. Glass was especially popular among the Crow because it was not made in their homeland and it could be used in many ways, including as a decoration for clothing, as a bauble to be worn on a strip of leather as a necklace, and, if polished properly, as a tool for starting fires.

But the trade items that the Crow most wanted were beads and musket balls. The beads that traders brought with them were made in Europe from glass of many different colors. The Crow used them to decorate nearly everything they owned: dresses, leggings, moccasins, leather tool bags, horse bridles, and saddles. The Crow soon learned to duplicate on these articles, in brightly colored beads, the designs they had previously painted, carved, or embroidered with dyed porcupine quills. Since Larocque first introduced the Crow to glass beads, the tribe's beadwork has become known as among the finest ever done in North America.

Musket balls were valued by the Crow, although they did not always prefer using guns instead of their traditional bows and arrows. When mounted on a swift pony in the midst of a buffalo herd, for instance, a warrior

A Crow quiver made of animal fur and decorated with multicolored beads. The tribe first obtained glass beads from non-Indian traders in the early 19th century.

found a bow easier to handle than a long-barreled gun. Of course, warriors in raiding parties also found it more effective to descend upon an unsuspecting enemy quietly with a bow and arrow rather than announce their presence with the flash and bang of a musket charge. But there was one task for which muskets were unsurpassed: killing people in battle. Muskets were powerful and could be used to hit a human target from a great distance. Guns were a favored trade item among all Plains Indians because no tribe could afford to allow its neighbor to accumulate more weapons than it had. Like the populations of modern nations that worry if their enemies have more missiles or battleships, the Crow were afraid to let the Blackfoot or the Sioux get ahead of them in musket power.

It is telling that Larocque traded musket *balls* rather than muskets themselves to the Crow. This indicates that sometime before the tribe's first recorded encounter with a white trader, it had acquired guns either from Indian merchants (possibly among the Knife River Hidatsa) or from another white trader. The Hidatsa had probably received their first guns from Canadians and Canadian-allied Indians who brought them to the Plains in the 1700s. In fact, the Crow had probably already seen most of the goods Larocque gave them, either at the Hidatsa villages or during meetings with neighboring tribes or wandering non-Indians who did not write diaries like Larocque's about their experiences with the tribe.

Larocque, however, was the first trader to give the Crow large quantities of these items in order to set up long-term trade with them.

Early non-Indian traders brought the Crow something else that changed their life even more than trade goods—European diseases. Although the Crow were still a large and powerful tribe when Larocque visited them in 1805, he noted that their population had been decimated by a succession of smallpox epidemics that had swept the Plains during the previous two or three decades. North American Indians had never been exposed to smallpox, measles, and many other diseases until they came in contact with non-Indians who were infected with them. The Crow, therefore, had not built up immunities against smallpox and were especially susceptible to the virus that caused the disease. Exactly when smallpox epidemics began and how deadly they were among the Crow is difficult to estimate. According to Larocque, they had reduced the number of people in the tribe from 16,000 to 2,400. He may have overestimated the disease's impact, but other observers confirm that the Crow suffered a dramatic population loss. The tribe was hit particularly hard because infectious diseases were easily transmitted in the close quarters of the lodges where the Crow lived during the winter months. Their traditional healing practices, which included sweat baths and fasting, could also make people already ill with smallpox even worse. As the Crow's contact with non-

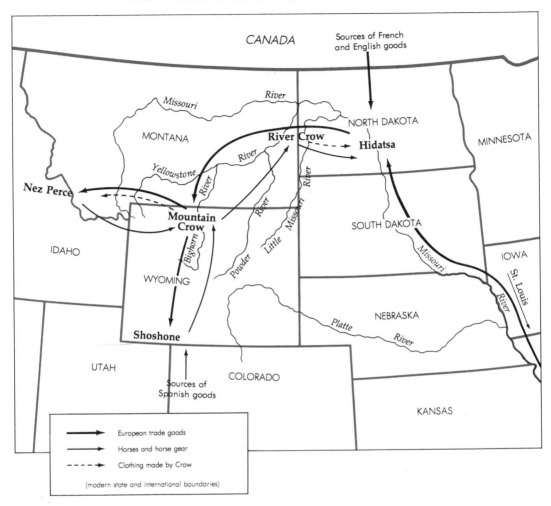

Indians increased over the next several decades, European diseases would remain a problem for the tribe.

A year after Larocque's summer among the Crow, a group of explorers traveled through Crow country. This expedition had been sent west in 1803 by President Thomas Jefferson. Jefferson's orders came on the heels of the United States's purchase of the Louisiana Territory from France. This huge tract of approximately 800,000 square miles of land between the Mississippi River and the Rocky Mountains included the Crow homeland. Its acquisition nearly doubled the size of the country. Curious about this uncharted land and its inhabitants, and eager for information about a possible water route from the Mississippi to the Pacific Ocean, the president entrusted the mission of exploring the region to two experienced soldiers and frontiersmen, Meriwether Lewis and William Clark, along with 43 companions. In the spring of 1806 half of this party, led by Clark, traveled down the Yellowstone River. They saw the Crow's buffalo herds but did not encounter the tribe's warriors.

Late in the summer, the members of the Lewis and Clark expedition reunited and floated down the Missouri River on their return trip east. En route one adventurer, a middle-aged Virginian named John Colter, asked his commanders for permission to double back upriver. Colter knew the expedition had been a success and was itching to see more of the Rockies and to try his hand at fur trading. His superiors agreed, and Colter headed upriver in the fall of 1806 with some traders he had met at the villages of the Mandan Indians, where the expedition had spent the previous winter. Before Lewis and Clark were able to travel to Washington, D.C., to report to President Jefferson about their journey, Colter was already ranging the Yellowstone Valley. He spent the winter of 1806–7 along the banks of the river. The next summer he went into business with Manuel Lisa, a Spanish-American businessman who founded the Missouri River Fur Trading Company of St. Louis. Lisa had heard of Clark's glowing description of the abundant wildlife along the upper Missouri and rushed to the region in order to beat his competitors to this rich source of beaver furs.

Colter, Lisa, and several other partners decided to erect a building at the mouth of the Bighorn River from which they could trade with the Crow year-round. This building—the first frame structure in present-day Montana—was called Fort Raymond. (This "fort" was actually a two-room log cabin.) In 1807 and 1808, Colter and the other traders pushed farther into the Crow's hunting grounds. There they discovered rich trapping areas and other places where the tribe gathered to visit and trade among themselves.

One of the most successful of these early traders was Edward Rose, a powerfully built man of white, black, and Cherokee descent. Rose learned that generosity was the key to becoming a friend of the Crow. Rather than barter with them for the best deal, Rose began his trading relationship with the Indians in 1808 by giving presents to all the important village chiefs. When Rose's boss Manuel Lisa learned that he was giving away company property without getting furs in return, he was furious. Rose quit, packed up his belongings, took all the goods from Lisa's company that he could, and left to live with his new Crow friends. Rose was one of the first of these early mountain men to decide that life with the Crow was preferable to that in the more settled and "civilized" eastern United States. Although he had some contact with white traders after 1808, he lived most of his remaining years with a Crow woman he married and her family.

Manuel Lisa abandoned Fort Raymond in 1811, but traders continued to flock to Crow territory. In the years that followed, the Yellowstone country was crisscrossed by dozens of traders who were not employed by large fur companies. Most of these men were illiterate and therefore could not leave a written record of their adventures. Even if they had been able to write, they probably would not have done so because they would not want to reveal to other traders the location of choice trapping areas or the names of their most reliable Indian trading partners. But after they returned east, several mountain men told their stories—often stretched to tall-tale proportions. Among these were Zenas Leonard, a Pennsylvanian who spent the winter of 1832–33 with the Crow and observed their tobacco planting rituals; Charles Larpenteur, who traveled with the Crow through Wind River country in 1833; and James Beckwourth, a black fur trader who joined the Crow in 1825 and later claimed to have married a Crow woman and to have led his new kinsmen into battle.

Various "forts" were built in place of Fort Raymond near the mouth of the Bighorn between 1821 and 1852. Because fur traders usually operated independently and with few resources, these forts never existed for very long. (None was in operation for more than eight years.) Moreover, they had to compete with Fort Union, an actual fort erected by the American Fur Company

Manuel Lisa, a Spanish-American trader who helped to establish Fort Raymond, the first trading post in Crow country, in 1807.

at the confluence of the Yellowstone and Missouri rivers in 1829. Fort Union was the point from which many traders shipped to the east the furs they had obtained from the Crow and other Indians on the northern Plains. Mountain men also came together along the Sweetwater River to the south of Crow country for a rendezvous each spring. Here traders brought the furs they had collected during the previous winter and met with merchants from St. Louis. Carrying stores of goods to trade for pelts, these merchants traveled across the prairies of what is now Nebraska by following the north bank of the Platte

An 1833 painting by Karl Bodmer of Plains Indians gathering at Fort Union. From this post, American Fur Company traders shipped to the East the furs they had obtained from the Crow and other Indian tribes.

River to attend this event. This system of trade remained in place until 1837, when the steamboat *Yellowstone* first began to make regular stops at Fort Union. The event signaled the beginning of the end for the independent mountain man. The steamboat's steady schedule and great carrying capacity gave traders traveling on it a tremendous advantage over mountain men, whose inventory was limited to what they could carry on their backs or in canoes.

The same year also spelled the end of the Knife River villages where the Crow and the Hidatsa had once lived together. A smallpox epidemic swept through the settlements, leaving behind row upon row of empty lodges and almost more dead than the living could bury. The Hidatsa's location on the Missouri River, which served as the white man's "highway" in the early years of exploration, brought them in constant contact with non-Indians infected with the disease. In addition, the tribespeople spent most of the year in huge earth lodges, the perfect setting for catching and passing on illnesses.

Unlike their Hidatsa friends, the Crow survived renewed outbreaks of smallpox. Their population had even increased slightly after their initial exposure to the disease. Edwin Thompson Denig, a fur trader who knew the Crow for 30 years in the early 1800s, wrote that by 1856 their numbers had risen from less than 3,000 to nearly 4,000. By traveling in small groups and scattering in different directions as soon as an infection among them was discovered, the Crow were able to stop the spread of disease. The tribe was also partially isolated from new viruses because its members traveled along the upper Missouri River and in isolated hunting grounds near the Bighorn and Wind rivers. Here they had limited contact with white travelers and fur traders and consequently less chance of having diseases transmitted to them.

Despite these tactics that the Crow developed to ensure their survival, Denig predicted in the 1850s that the tribe would soon be extinct. "Situated as they now are," he wrote, "the Crows cannot exist long as a nation." Denig was not referring to the dangers of disease, however. Instead, he was observing the new dangers presented to them by other Indians, who had begun to compete fiercely with the tribe for the

A 19th-century engraving of the steamboat Yellowstone, *which first arrived at Fort Union in 1837.*

shrinking supply of beaver, buffalo, and land on the Plains. As more and more non-Indians flocked to the region, less and less of these resources were available to the Indians who lived there. The coming of the white man to the Plains was like an overweight man trying to enter a crowded elevator: As he pushes his way in, the passengers in the rear of the car are gradually squeezed against the wall. They cannot get off, so they end up with less space between themselves and their fellow riders.

The pressure on the Plains Indians came from all directions and increased as the years passed. The opening in 1847 of the Oregon Trail across present-day Nebraska and southern Wyoming, and the California gold rush of 1849

brought a flood of non-Indian travelers to the Plains. By 1850 wagon trains regularly crossed present-day southern Wyoming on their way to Oregon Territory and California. But aside from white traders and settlers headed for the Pacific Coast, most of the inhabitants of what are now North Dakota, South Dakota, Wyoming, Colorado, and Montana were Indians. However, in the eastern portions of the Great Plains, Indians, particularly the Sioux and Cheyenne, were being forced out of their territories by non-Indian settlers.

Rather than battling these intruders, with whom the Indians wanted to continue to trade for knives, guns, and other goods, the groups in the eastern Plains began to move into areas claimed

A sketch of an Awatixa village, drawn by Sitting Rabbit, a Hidatsa man. The village was deserted after a smallpox epidemic in 1837.

by other tribes. The Sioux traveled northward into the southern portion of Crow country to hunt along the Powder and Tongue rivers. White settlement in Oregon Territory and an increase in trade with non-Indians in present-day northwestern Montana caused the Blackfoot to encroach upon the Crow. The Blackfoot started to range near the headwaters of the Missouri and Yellowstone rivers, the western edge of the Crow homeland. As a result, the Crow grew extremely protective of their hunting areas. Whereas a century earlier they might have allowed a visit from a Sioux or Blackfoot band, in 1850 the appearance of strangers meant war.

With warfare between tribes mounting and the pace of white migration across the Plains quickening, United States officials decided in the summer of 1851 to gather representatives of all the Plains Indian tribes together to clarify their boundaries and to secure their promise to maintain peaceful relations with whites. At the officials' invitation, thousands of Crow, Sioux, Blackfoot, Shoshone, Cheyenne and others—the largest gathering of Plains Indians ever recorded—assembled at Fort Laramie near the headwaters of the Platte River to meet the U.S. government's representatives and settle their differences.

Beginning with Lewis and Clark in 1805, American officials who ventured onto the Plains had long been concerned with establishing which lands belonged to which tribes. In the East, Americans kept track of their property by drawing careful borders on maps and surveying precise boundaries between their farms and towns, so it seemed logical to them to do the same with the Indians' land. They believed, too, that clear borders would promote peace among the various tribes by giving each group an area of its own.

The Crow had previously negotiated a treaty with the United States in 1825. But it was simply a pledge of friendship intended as a guarantee that the Crow would not incite trouble on the nation's western border. Written long before white settlers began to move onto the northern Plains, the 1825 agreement did not establish any specific boundaries. The 1851 treaty did and therefore required more careful negotiation.

Although an honorable method of handling differences between sovereign peoples, treaty making put great pressure on Crow elders. They had to study and understand a document written in English, anticipate problems with the enforcement of its provisions, and gauge how far they could push the U.S. government's negotiators with their own demands. Despite these hurdles, the Crow leaders drove as hard a bargain as they could.

When the proceedings were over, the Crow had succeeded in defining their homeland on the government's maps. After 1851, Crow country was a specific area bounded on the east by the Powder River, on the west by the headwaters of the Yellowstone River, on the north by the Missouri and Musselshell rivers, and on the south by the Wind

An illustration of a warrior fighting two Sioux Indians, drawn on ledger paper by Crow chief Pretty Eagle in 1884. Warfare between the Crow and the Sioux increased during the 1850s as bands of Sioux began to encroach on Crow hunting territory.

River Mountains. Although this was a huge amount of land (approximately 38 million acres), it did not include the Little Missouri River and the surrounding region, which the Crow had previously shared with their Hidatsa relatives. It also did not include areas to the south and west where they had earlier hunted and traded with the Shoshone and Nez Perce Indians. The other tribes at Fort Laramie faced similar adjustments. They had not lost much land but, as they became aware of their territory's borders, they began to sense that unsettled land and the game and other resources it contained were growing more scarce.

In July 1806, William Clark had sat on the banks of Pryor Creek in the center of the Crow homeland and written, "For me to mention or give an estimate of the different species of wild animals on this river, particularly buffalo, elk, antelope, and wolves, would be incredible." A few days later Clark's party could not sleep because a huge herd of buffalo passed near them in the night. Only 50 years after Clark's visit, Edwin Thompson Denig wrote that the Yellowstone River region was still "the best game country in the world," but behind his words was a sense of doom rather than wonder. By this time, Crow country was no longer an isolated spot. Non-Indians such as Denig had been bringing new tools and weapons to the Indians for decades, thus helping to bring about important changes in their

Indian traders in the inner courtyard at Fort Laramie, painted by Alfred Jacob Miller in 1837.

world. What Clark had marveled over in 1806 had been a magnet to mountain men, fur traders, settlers, and other Indians. These people had rushed to Bighorn country, many hoping to cash in on the riches of this environment. In a brief period of time, the tribe had become surrounded by newcomers.

With all of these changes, it is not surprising that the Crow's first 50 years of contact with non-Indians produced a new type of chief. In the past, men had become leaders by demonstrating skill at hunting and staging raids on enemies. Because the Crow believed these talents flowed from the Creator, they also thought successful leaders had special religious powers. Following the arrival of fur traders, other skills were added to the qualifications for a Crow chief. Hunting and raiding were still essential, but leaders also needed to demonstrate an ability to trade with non-Indians and to adapt to the many unexpected events that seemed to accompany the arrival of the white man.

Eelapuash had all of these qualities. Called Sore Belly by some, Eelapuash was a tall, muscular man who was born about the time of the American Revolution. He was not very friendly (some explorers reported that he was always cranky), but he had the respect of his many followers.

Eelapuash was a River Crow. He loved to visit his Hidatsa friends, parading into their Missouri River villages wearing a beautiful beaded shirt and leading a long procession of Crow warriors. One early explorer who met him among the Hidatsa recalled his impression of Eelapuash when the leader invited him into the lodge where he was staying: "A small fire in the center gave sufficient light. The chief sat opposite the entrance and around him many fine tall men, placed according to their rank, all with no other covering than a breech cloth." He invited his visitors to smoke tobacco and take in his grandeur.

But Eelapuash was much more than a showman. He was an extraordinary warrior who had led war parties from a very early age and almost always returned with horses or scalps. When surrounded by enemies, he thought nothing of leaping from his horse and rushing their forces armed only with a tomahawk. By the time Larocque arrived among the Crow, Eelapuash was well respected for his military genius.

When the fur trade era began, Eelapuash advised his followers to pass up trinkets in favor of ammunition and tools. He knew that the Crow's enemies were quickly accumulating their own piles of weapons, so he also insisted that the Crow improve their system of posting sentinels. Perhaps most importantly, Eelapuash taught his men to use their new weapons to launch fierce campaigns against anyone who dared trifle with the Crow.

On one occasion, he led a specially selected war party far to the south—perhaps to present-day Kansas—to pursue a group of Cheyenne who had ambushed some unsuspecting Crow. Eelapuash commanded the army and promised to follow his enemies as far

A 19th-century shield made of painted rawhide that belonged to a Crow man named Wraps Up His Tail (also known as Sword Bearer).

as what is now New Mexico in order to avenge the loss of his friends. Another time, he struck against the Blackfoot, leading a war party across present-day Montana and laying siege to a fur trader's fort where the enemy had obtained their weapons. Eelapuash failed in that campaign because the defenders of the fort were able to hold on until reinforcements arrived to drive the Crow away.

Eelapuash died in a battle in 1834 when he tried to defeat 20 Blackfoot warriors single-handedly. But he was succeeded by others who, although not as fierce as he, felt as greatly the burdens of a chief's responsibilities. Among these was a Mountain Crow named Long Hair (also known as Red Plume). Unlike Eelapuash, he signed the treaty of friendship between the Crow and the United States in 1825. Known for never having cut his hair (on special occasions he would unwrap it from the coil in which he normally wore it and allow it to trail on the ground), Long Hair lived until about 1850.

In the 1850s, Big Robber and Twines His Tail were two of the most prominent Crow leaders. Each was skilled not only in hunting and warfare but also in trading with mountain men and speaking with representatives of the U.S. government. A Mountain Crow, Big Robber spent most of his life south of the Bighorn Mountains, where he traded with trappers who gathered near the Wind River Mountains. He was a successful war leader and recognized by the U.S. government as the tribe's spokesman at official meetings and negotiations. This association with the United States also cost him, however. Many Crow refused to follow Big Robber when they came to believe he represented the white man's point of view. Despite this loss of prestige in his later years, Big Robber died gloriously in battle in 1858.

Twines His Tail was a River Crow. He looked to the American Fur Company's post at Fort Union for his sup-

Crow leader Red Bear, drawn by George Catlin in 1832.

plies and tended to spend most of his time in the Yellowstone River valley to the north of the Bighorns. Like Big Robber, Twines His Tail was an accomplished war leader who drew part of his authority from his position as a speaker at meetings with representatives of the United States. He negotiated with them on behalf of his people and received the government's payments of food and clothing for distribution among the Crow.

The necessity for chiefs such as Big Robber and Twines His Tail to deal effectively with traders and government men is made strikingly clear in a journal entry of Rudolph Kurz, a Swiss painter who spent several years near the Crow in the early 1850s. Kurz reported that Twines His Tail visited him one day at Fort Union and was terribly upset because some presents that the government had promised to give the Crow had not arrived. Twines His Tail was angry not because the United States had broken its promises or because he feared his people might suffer from the delay. Instead, he was perturbed by the thought that the presents might be shipped up the Platte River to Big Robber rather than up the Missouri to him. Twines His Tail explained to Kurz that if the items came up the Platte, Big Robber would be able to distribute them to the Crow. He would then become the chief of the tribe and Twines His Tail's followers would desert him.

There were several other men—including Two Face, Bear's Head, Red Bear, and Iron Bull—who held important positions during these early years of white contact. The Crow continued to look to more than one leader to represent them. But, as whites and other Indians encroached on their lands more and more, they only chose chiefs who could defend the Crow homeland, bargain with traders, and speak to white men across a council fire.

The coming of the white man had brought many changes—new tools, new diseases, and new ideas. In the past, the Crow had had much experience adjusting to change and making the most of new opportunities. However, living with non-Indians placed enormous demands on the tribe that challenged its ability to adapt to the unfamiliar. But just as the Crow had mastered the art of living on the Great Plains, learned to ride ponies, and became proficient at firing muskets, so they were able to develop ways of sharing their homeland with strangers. ▲

Medicine Crow, photographed in the late 19th century.

THE
HIGH TIDE
OF CHANGE

Many Plains Indians have a saying: "Only the hills last forever." This is certainly known by the Crow, for whom life has never been quiet or settled. Throughout their history, they have always accepted change as a fact of their existence. But during the late 1800s, the burdens placed on them by their rapidly changing world were unique.

In the space of 50 years, most of the "permanent" features of Crow life disappeared. Hunting, which had provided their livelihood for more than 100 years, became impossible as fewer and fewer buffalo and other game roamed through their territory. The Plains, which had always been open to bands of traveling Crow, were suddenly fenced by non-Indians, plowed up by farmers, and crossed by railroad tracks. And all of the Indian people in the area—friends, allies, and enemies alike—became a minority in their own home as the wave of settlers from Eu-

rope and the eastern United States continued to arrive in the region. In the second half of the 19th century, change reached high tide, and when the tide receded the Crow were in a new world.

After the Civil War (1861–64), thousands of Americans fled the East to seek their fortune on the Plains. Many came to work on the construction of railroads that would connect eastern cities, such as Chicago and St. Louis with present-day California, Oregon, and Washington state. Others flocked to present-day North and South Dakota, Montana, and Idaho in search of gold. In Montana Territory, the discovery of the mineral in the early 1860s had created the boomtowns of Bozeman and Virginia City, where businessmen stocked their shelves in anticipation of new migrations of greenhorns as word of the gold strikes spread farther east. Still others traveled west to stake a claim to farmland or just to explore the region.

All of these newcomers frightened and angered the Indians whose lands had been "guaranteed" to be safe from encroachment by the treaties negotiated at Fort Laramie in 1851. Among the most powerful—and the most irritated—of these Indians were the Lakota, the western division of Sioux whose hunting grounds lay directly in the path of the westward-bound settlers. The Lakota had felt pressured by migrations from the east as early as the 1600s. Their Indian neighbors in present-day Minnesota, the Ojibwa, obtained guns from French traders and began using them to expand their hunting grounds. By the time of the American Revolution, the Ojibwa's ferocity and the attraction of buffalo hunting drew the Lakota onto the central Plains. As settlers moved into the Kansas and Nebraska territories in the 1850s, the tribe ranged farther and farther northwest to hunt. Eventually they began to move into Bighorn country, hunting and raiding in the Crow homeland.

During the summer of 1866, the Lakota responded to the white advance by declaring war on a series of forts that the U.S. army was constructing along the Bozeman Trail, a wagon road that ran from Fort Laramie to the Montana goldfields. The trail soon earned the nickname "the Bloody Bozeman" because of the Sioux raids. Red Cloud, a great Lakota chief, visited the Crow's villages and urged their young warriors to join his force's attacks, but the Crow declined.

Fort C. F. Smith, the westernmost fort on the Bozeman Trail, was erected on the east bank of the Bighorn River nearly 400 miles from Fort Laramie during the summer of 1866. Among the 165 U.S. soldiers assigned to Fort Smith was Lieutenant William Templeton, a 24-year-old Civil War veteran from Pennsylvania. As Templeton and his comrades nervously took up their posts, they scanned the surrounding peaks and forests for signs of hostile Indians. They knew they were outnumbered and prayed that their cannon would help them survive the fighting that was sure to come. They knew, too, that they were defending the most isolated and vulnerable outpost in the United States.

At the end of August, Templeton recorded in his diary that a group of warriors appeared on the other side of the Bighorn River and began shouting at the soldiers. With rifles ready, Templeton and a detachment of soldiers left the fort and rode out to meet the mounted and well-armed Indians. Templeton did not know any Indian languages, but when he heard the word *Absaroka*, he relaxed. These Indians were Crow, and they had come not to attack the fort but to trade and visit.

The next day a group of soldiers, including Templeton and the colonel in command of Fort Smith, met with the Crow chiefs. Surprisingly, the Indians did not scold the bluejackets—as the soldiers were known because of the color of their uniforms—for building an unauthorized fort on Crow territory. Instead, the Crow welcomed them to the Bighorn Valley. They reported that 1,500 Sioux were camped nearby on the Tongue River and that Sioux warriors had been stealing their horses and pestering the tribe to join them in war against the United States. The colonel was firm. He declared that the Crow should remain loyal and assured them that the U.S. Army would defeat the Sioux. Afterwards, the colonel told them, whites and friendly Indians like themselves would live together in peace. "How, How!" the chiefs replied, jumping to their feet and vigorously shaking hands with the startled soldiers. Templeton later reported that one of the Crow, a short, muscular man named Boy Chief, then threw his arms around the young lieutenant, playfully snatched the officer's cap from his head, and made a short speech. The army's Indian interpreter quickly told Templeton that the chief said he loved him and hoped his love would be returned. Boy Chief then repeated these words to every officer present.

This scene reminds us that the Indian wars on the Plains during the 1860s and 1870s were not simply battles between whites and Indians. The conflicts did not always pit Indians against non-Indians who sought to "win the West" for civilization. The story of the Crow during this era of violence is that of a group trying to protect its territory from a variety of enemies, which included other Indians as well as white miners, settlers, and soldiers.

A group of Crow men who served as scouts for the U.S. Army during the 1870s.

As Boy Chief and his friends demonstrated, the Crow had enemies who seemed to them more dangerous than U.S. troops. They were surrounded by tribes who were pushing into their homeland in an effort to get away from the path of both migrating settlers and the railroads. The tribe was suspicious of the army as well as white prospectors, farmers, and cattlemen, but it never went to war with the United States. As U.S. allies, many Crow served as army scouts and couriers.

The first page of the 1868 treaty between the Crow and the United States, in which the tribe agreed to cede almost 30 million acres of its territory.

They followed this course, however, because they believed they were defending their own best interests. They did not decide to join the "good" side or the "bad" side of these battles; their goal was to remain on the Crow side.

Warfare had always been an important part of Crow life, and it was to remain so during the Plains fighting. Young men proved their worth by capturing horses and raiding enemy villages. Other warriors proved the power of their ties to the supernatural by leading war parties. The community Sun Dance—still a central feature of the tribe's religious life—continued to be held to help warriors exact revenge upon the Crow's enemies. However, the meaning and nature of warfare changed. Wars were no longer a series of small raids with little impact on the tribe's general welfare. Instead, they were now fought with deadly weapons, and their outcome had important, long-term consequences for the tribe.

The Crow came to see that by winning or losing a battle, a group won or lost important resources, such as access to areas with large beaver populations, government gifts, and sources of weapons. Such results affected more than a young man's reputation or the prestige of a holy man. Crow Indians such as Boy Chief understood that most of their Indian enemies had been pushed out of their homes by white settlers elsewhere in the United States, and looked to American officials to rescue them from the onslaught of these migrants.

The Crow stuck to this strategy throughout the battles on the Bozeman Trail. Some men worked for the army; others chose to be neutral and simply withdrew into the Bighorn Mountains and remained there until the fighting was over. In 1868 the United States admitted defeat against Red Cloud's warriors. In a peace treaty signed at Fort

Laramie, the government agreed to abandon the U.S. Army's outposts on the trail, including Fort Smith. The treaty also guaranteed the Sioux possession of their lands west of the Missouri River (including the Black Hills) and ensured that they would still be able to hunt buffalo in the Powder River valley due east of Crow country.

The Crow and several other Plains tribes also attended the 1868 peace council at Fort Laramie. Sits in the Middle of the Land, a powerful 70-year-old Mountain Crow leader, spoke for the tribe at these proceedings. Fearing that his people would eventually lose all their land otherwise, he accepted a substantial reduction in the tribe's territory on the condition that the U.S. government establish a permanent Crow homeland and guarantee them the right to hunt in unoccupied areas of the Plains. When the negotiations were complete, Sits in the Middle of the Land had succeeded in achieving his major objectives. The 1868 treaty signed by the Crow recognized the Bighorn Valley as the Crow domain. However, it also cleared nearly 30 million acres, granted them by the treaty of 1851, for non-Indian settlement and for the route of the Union Pacific Railroad. This agreement thus sealed the fate of the buffalo on the Plains. The new rail line would split the huge western herd into two parts and make it easier for hunters to reach the animals. (They could now even do their hunting from an open window on a train.)

The 1851 treaty had recognized the Crow's claim to much of the tribe's traditional hunting and trapping areas. As a result, it did little to restrict the Crow's movements. The 1868 treaty, however, reduced the tribe's territory to an 8-million-acre area bounded on the south by the northern boundary of Wyoming Territory (the 45th degree parallel), on the east by the 107th degree longitude, and on the north and west by the Yel-

Crow chief Sits in the Middle of the Land (center), who spoke for the tribe during the negotiation of its 1868 treaty, and two other Crow leaders, Long Horse (left) and White Calf (right), in an 1873 photograph.

lowstone River. Not only did this deprive the Crow of most of their land but it also restricted them to a region whose boundaries they did not understand. The southern and eastern borders were straight lines drawn on the government's maps that had no meaning to the Crow. The effect of the treaty, therefore, was merely to confine the tribe to a wedge of land south of the Yellowstone River. They were permitted to follow their old hunting paths north of Yellowstone or south into Wind River country only as long as these trips did not interfere with non-Indian settlement.

Although the Crow gave a huge amount of territory to the United States in the 1868 agreement, the Montana Territory legislature petitioned Congress for further reductions in the size of the tribe's domain immediately after the treaty was signed. More gold had been discovered at Clark's Fork on the Yellowstone River; hence, prospectors were eager to enter the Crow's western lands. In addition, non-Indian businessmen in the East planned to run the lines of the Northern Pacific Railroad straight through the Yellowstone Valley and wanted to get the Crow out of its way. Despite the pressure these miners and industrialists placed on the local government, the Crow would be able to hold onto the territory guaranteed them in 1868 for several more decades.

The Sioux, however, soon experienced problems with the federal gov-

(continued on page 81)

Crow Indians gathered in 1883 to witness the driving of the last spike into the rails of the Northern Pacific Railroad.

SHIELDS OF POWER

Objects have different meanings in different settings. A baseball cap worn to a game on a summer afternoon is a symbol of loyalty and good cheer. The same hat worn by a shabby man on a winter morning in a big city communicates poverty and despair. As this lesson suggests, the shields the Crow Indians made more than a century ago cannot be fully appreciated today without an understanding of what they meant to the warriors who carried them into battle.

The Crow made their shields from rawhide. These disks were tough, but their owners knew that animal skin alone could not protect them from their enemies' weapons. They believed the shields were far stronger than the materials from which they were made. This added strength came from spiritual power, the same power that the Crow believed had created the earth.

The decorations on a man's shield revealed to the world his connection to the Creator. These sometimes included symbols of things he had seen in a vision. Such visions often gave young Crow men the confidence to become warriors. A shield might also have sacred objects, such as feathers, attached to it. Thus, when a Crow warrior took up his shield, he was actually arming himself with a power that he believed would make him invincible.

Today most Crow shields are preserved in museums. On display in an age of missiles and nuclear bombs, they may appear to be nothing more than circles of painted animal skin. The meaning of their markings, however, indicate otherwise. They reveal the union that the Crow people have always felt with their Creator and of the power it has given them.

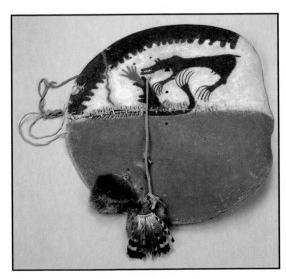

A Crow shield painted with an image of one bear attacking another that has a human hand emerging from its mouth.

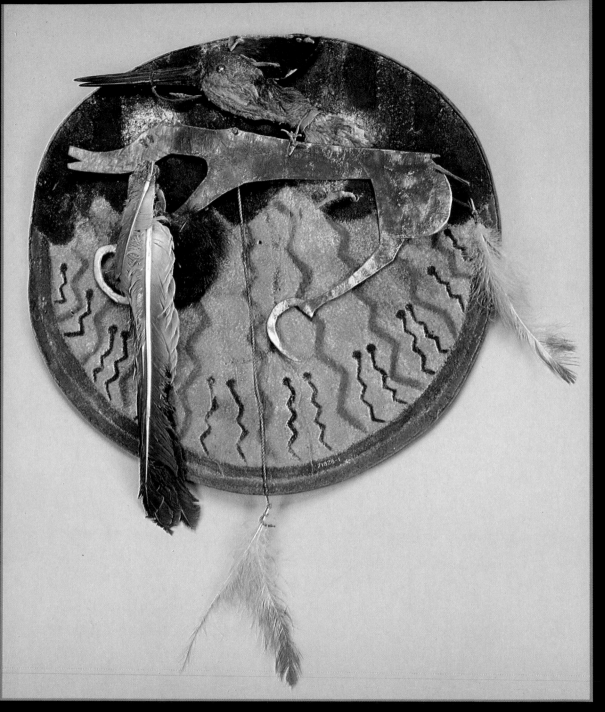

A storm cloud emitting lightning bolts is painted on this shield, which belonged to a warrior named Bull Snake. The black lines at the bottom represent bullets shooting skyward. The eagle feathers, crane's head, and piece of rawhide in the shape of a buffalo gave special strength to the shield's owner.

Passed down through five generations, this shield was last owned by Spotted Rabbit. The 10 heavy stripes represent scalps taken in battle; the blackened portion to the left is a thundercloud. At the bottom of the shield, a buffalo bull is shown pursuing a buffalo cow into the cloud.

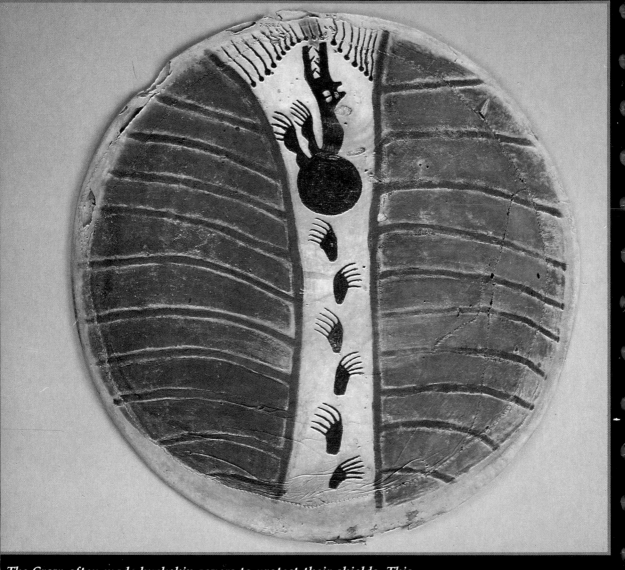

The Crow often made buckskin covers to protect their shields. This cover is painted with a scene of an angry bear being shot by 19 bullets as it rushes from its den toward its attacker. According to the shield's owner, Big Bear, the green half of the cover represents the earth, and the red half, the sky.

71725-2

Bull That Goes Hunting made this shield to represent his vision of a giant buffalo bull standing astride the Pryor Mountains as it defies its enemies. Three bullet holes testify that the shield was used in battle.

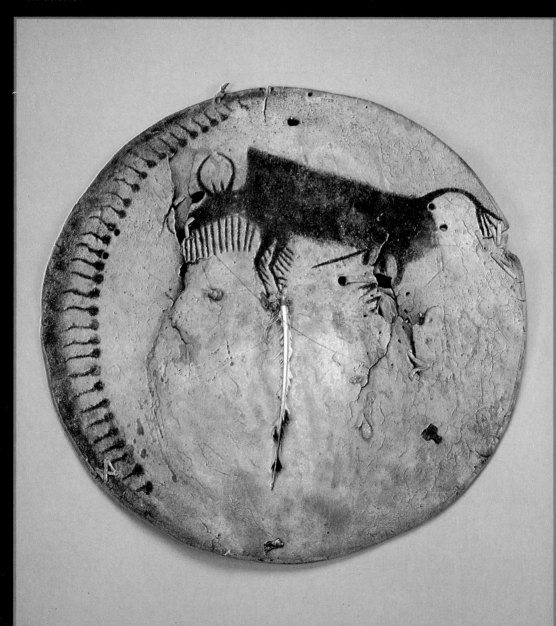

This shield originally belonged to Eelapuash (Sore Belly), one of the greatest Crow warriors. Attached to it are two squirrel skins to make Eelapuash quick, a weasel skin to make him watchful, and several eagle feathers to give him power.

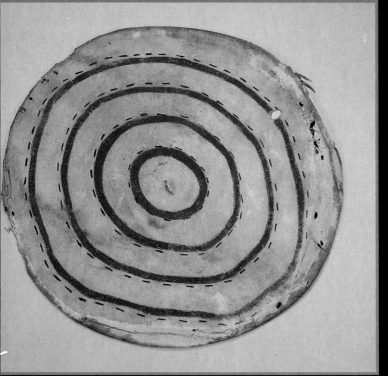

A man named Kiss owned this shield. Its four red circles represent sun dogs—the circles that appear around the sun before a storm. The black lines are pieces of a man that are so small his enemies cannot touch him.

Bull Tongue carried this shield into many battles against the Sioux. The four red crane tracks ensured that this bird would protect him.

(continued from page 72)

ernment's refusal to honor its promises. Despite the provisions of the 1868 treaty, the United States continued to send troops into Sioux territory, especially after gold was discovered in the Black Hills. In turn, the Sioux violated the agreement by attacking these intruders. In 1876, Sioux power crested when the tribe's warriors killed General George Armstrong Custer and the soldiers of the Seventh Cavalry whom he commanded at the Battle of Little Bighorn. Several Crow rode with Custer's doomed contingent as scouts but, as was customary with Indians in those positions, they were discharged by the young colonel before the fighting began. (Two tribesman, however, did fight with Major Marcus Reno's detachment, which survived the battle.) Most of the Crow were neutral, and the government continued to recognize the tribe's ownership of their old hunting ground.

Today, a white marble monument stands atop a windy hill overlooking the valley of the Little Bighorn River. It marks the spot where Custer and his men fell before a combined force of Sioux and Cheyenne warriors on June 25, 1876. For thousands of tourists who visit the monument every year, it is a tribute to the bravery of Custer and his men and to the tactical brilliance of Crazy Horse, Two Moon, and the others who defeated the American soldiers there. A third group can also be said to be honored by the monument, even though their dead are not buried there and they are not mentioned on the roadside markers. These people are the Crow, who still occupy the site of Custer's last stand. The strategy they developed for dealing with the U.S. government allowed them to survive that day when so many soldiers and warriors died in terror.

After the Battle of Little Bighorn, the army pursued Sitting Bull and the other Sioux chiefs and forced them to return to Sioux lands in Dakota Territory. The Crow then reoccupied the portion of their lands that the Sioux had encroached upon during the previous two decades. The tribe hoped that finally it could live in peace.

However, only a year later, Looking Glass, a Nez Perce war chief and an old friend of the Crow, asked the tribe to go into battle with his followers. Following several skirmishes between the Nez Perce and U.S. troops led by General Oliver Howard, Looking Glass and his men were struggling to fend off the army long enough to escape across the Canadian border to safety. The Crow were tempted to come to their aid, but they decided once again not to oppose the United States. They did not want the army to be able to use charges of disloyalty as an excuse for depriving them of more of their territory.

Threatened on all sides and faced with enemies more powerful than any they had ever seen, the Crow's leaders marched through the whirlwind of the Plains wars on a steady course. Some were neutral and some were loyal to the army, but all were dedicated to keeping their homeland. With this goal always foremost in their minds, the Crow were one of the few tribes not to suffer greatly as a result of the Plains war era.

Yet the Crow's cooperation with the U.S. government did lead directly to many changes in their traditional way of life. When the Crow leaders signed the 1868 treaty, they agreed to more than a new set of boundaries for their territory. They also accepted a series of promises from the government. In exchange for the Crow's forfeit of 30 million acres of land, federal officials offered to provide the tribe with the services of several people—a carpenter, a miller, an engineer, a farmer, a blacksmith, a physician, and a schoolteacher—who would help them prepare for life in Montana Territory, which was becoming increasingly settled and "civilized." They also promised to build schools on the Crow's territory, supplement their food supply, and give them free tools. Perhaps most significant was the 1868 treaty's provision that these goods and services would be coordinated by a type of official previously unknown to the Crow—an agent. Unlike other government representatives who visited the tribe occasionally to distribute presents or to trade, the agent would be a permanent resident of Crow country. His responsibilities would also include attempting to help the Crow blend into American mainstream culture by persuading them to adopt the ways of the non-Indian settlers around them.

The tribe's first agent, Captain E. M. Camp, located his office (the agency) near present-day Livingston, Montana, on the western end of the tribe's lands. From the agency, he annually dispensed supplies of food, blankets, and tools to each Crow and tried to keep the tribe free from disturbance by prospectors and Sioux raiders. By 1873, when Camp left his post, his agency had proven both too vulnerable to Sioux and Blackfoot attacks and too isolated from most of the Crow, who lived farther to the east and north.

His successor, Fellows D. Pease, proposed moving the agency farther northwest to the Judith River basin in the center of Montana Territory. Pease won approval for his idea from the Crow, but politicians in both Montana Territory and Washington, D.C., initially rejected it. In an effort to "civilize" the tribe, Pease encouraged the Crow to farm as their non-Indian neighbors did, but he reported to his superiors that the land near the agency was too mountainous to produce good crops.

In 1875, Pease's request to move the agency was approved. It was relocated in the Stillwater River valley near Absaroka, Montana. The new agency was surrounded by rich, but not plentiful, farmland. Pease's successors spent the next decade trying to coax the Crow to become farmers, but most wanted to continue their old way of life. Following the defeat of the Sioux in 1876–77, the Crow could venture onto the nearby Plains without fear, but they found that buffalo and other game on which their traditional culture had depended were rapidly disappearing. Each fall hunting

CROW LAND CESSIONS IN THE 19TH AND 20TH CENTURIES

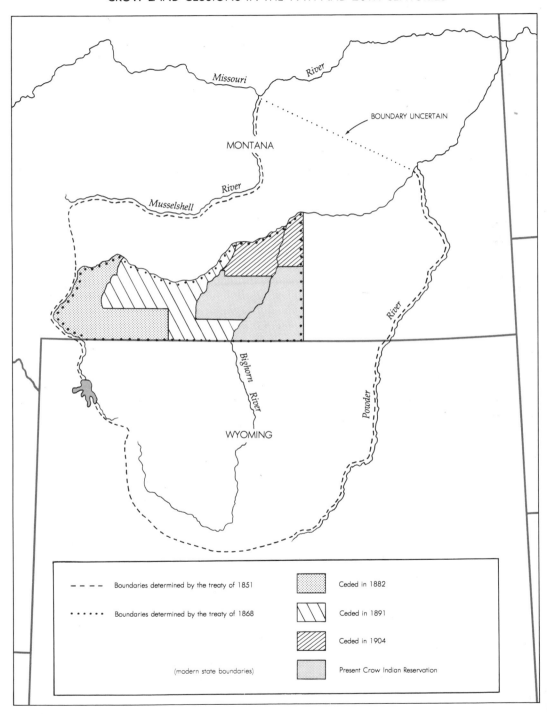

Missouri River

BOUNDARY UNCERTAIN

MONTANA

River

Musselshell

Bighorn River

Powder River

WYOMING

- – – – Boundaries determined by the treaty of 1851

· · · · · Boundaries determined by the treaty of 1868

(modern state boundaries)

Ceded in 1882

Ceded in 1891

Ceded in 1904

Present Crow Indian Reservation

Women at Crow Agency, Montana, receiving rations of meat from government officials in 1895.

bands would leave the agency in search of game, but they would usually return at Christmas to collect their annual food rations and government payments promised by the treaty of 1868. While they were there, the government agent usually persuaded a few children to attend a tiny school near the agency and tried to convince families to remain at Absaroka when the bands set off in the spring to hunt.

The government dealt a blow to the Crow who still preferred to travel the Plains when it asked the tribe to accept still another reduction in its territory.

Montana territorial officials had long been urging officials in Washington, D.C., to take over more tribal land. In 1880, a delegation of six Crow chiefs (including Iron Bull, Medicine Crow, and Plenty Coups) was summoned to the nation's capital to hear the arguments of government representatives who encouraged them to sell part of Crow country. The delegation was granted an audience with the commissioner who headed the Bureau of Indian Affairs, the federal agency formed to oversee relations between Indians and the U.S. government. They also had a brief conversation with President Rutherford B. Hayes. But in the end the chiefs could do little to prevent the loss of another tract of land. While in Washington, the Crow delegates agreed to sell 1.5 million acres in the western portion of their territory and granted the Northern Pacific Railroad a 400-foot-wide path along the southern bank of the Yellowstone River. In return the tribe was to receive $25,000 for granting the railroad right-of-way and $30,000 annually for 25 years for the land it ceded. Congress approved the sale on July 10, 1882.

As had been the case in 1868, however, the reduction in Crow territory stimulated, rather than satisfied, the desire for Crow land among non-Indians on the Plains. As the Northern Pacific's rail lines reached the border of Montana Territory, the railroad brought more settlers into the region. This influx of non-Indians caused merchants and politicians to look longingly at the unoccupied prairies that were still under tribal control.

In the meantime, the Crow gradually began to grow more comfortable with the agency on the Stillwater River. In the early 1870s, Wolf Bow, a warrior who had regularly visited and traded at Fort Smith in 1866 and 1867, was the first member of the tribe to settle permanently at the agency and attempt to farm there. Others soon decided to try their hand at farming, including Iron Bull, Medicine Crow, and Plenty Coups. These chiefs had proven themselves in battle according to Crow tradition, but had become convinced that it was time for the tribe to learn new ways. In 1883 the Crow agent reported that there was "a much larger number of Indians who were anxious to farm this season" than ever before. That year the Crow planted 125 acres of potatoes and, working in 2 crews under the direction of chiefs Plenty Coups and Pretty Eagle, earned $150 cutting hay for the agency's barns.

The American government forced a dramatic change on the Crow in 1884. After the tribe had suffered years of uncertain crops and conflicts with non-Indian settlers, its agent, army captain Henry J. Armstrong, insisted that all Crow move out of the mountains and take up farming. Armstrong led 100 Crows out of Stillwater country and onto the floor of the Little Bighorn Valley, a place he believed would be their springboard to "civilization." There they established the town of Crow Agency as a permanent headquarters for the tribe. With this move back to their old hunting grounds—now empty of buffalo—the Crow were brought face to face with a new way of life.

Many changes were introduced to the Crow by a pair of most unlikely visitors who arrived in Crow country in 1881. Father Pierpaolo Prando, a Catholic missionary of the Jesuit order, was dispatched there by his superiors at the St. Ignatius mission in western Montana Territory. Prando was Italian and had been in the United States for only two years. Although the Crow had met missionaries from time to time during the previous 50 years, Prando and his companion, Father Peter Barcelo, were the first churchmen to come and live with the tribe and to commit themselves to converting the Crow to Christianity.

It is difficult to imagine the Crow's response to Father Prando. Crow men tended to be tall, very athletic, and valued action; the priest was short, wore a robe and steel-rimmed glasses, and was a retiring bookworm. Despite their differences, Prando continued his association with the Crow for 25 years. He founded the St. Xavier mission in 1887 on the banks of the Bighorn River, became familiar enough with the Crow

Members of the Crow delegation that traveled to Washington, D.C., to negotiate the tribe's 1880 land cession. **Seated:** *Old Crow, Medicine Crow, Long Elk, Plenty Coups, and Pretty Eagle.* **Standing:** *interpreter A. M. Quivly, Two Belly, Agent Augustus R. Keller, and interpreter Tom Stewart.*

A Crow camp surrounding St. Xavier mission in 1890. The photograph was taken by Father Pierpaolo Prando, who founded the mission.

language to translate a number of hymns and scriptures, and urged the tribe to follow the teachings of the Catholic church. Many Crow listened to Prando because he took the time to learn their language and was willing to live within their community. Although they found the priest's way of life odd (Crow men had difficulty imagining life without marriage), they respected Prando because, unlike their agents and other government men, he could not be pressured or bribed. The Crow always appreciated newcomers who were honest and dedicated to helping them even if their ideas seemed strange and foolish.

Although encouraged by the Crow's agents, church attendance was not mandatory on the reservation. Likewise, farming was endorsed by government officials as the best way to make a living, but it was not forced on the Crow. The new government schools, however, were one "civilizing" force that the Crow could neither avoid nor ignore. Beginning with the tribe's move to the Little Bighorn Valley in 1884, Crow children over the age of six were required to attend a school built near the agency. During the following decade, day schools were built in other communities across the reservation, and boarding schools were established at Crow Agency, Pryor, and St. Xavier. Some Crow students were sent to other boarding schools in present-day Oregon, Oklahoma, Kansas, and even as

Crow students in 1896. After 1884, Crow children over the age of six were required to attend an agency school, where they were forced to adopt non-Indian ways.

far away as Pennsylvania. Teachers at all of these schools conducted their lessons in English.

Life for Crow children attending boarding schools was harsh. Students lived at these institutions and therefore were separated from their parents for long periods of time. Teachers forced them to abandon their traditional ways and adopt non-Indian dress and manners. The routine was grim. Children wore uniforms, worked in the school kitchens and laundries, and followed an almost military schedule in which an activity was planned for every moment of the day. Even worse, boarding schools were often so unsanitary that children became ill and infected other students. Physically weak children often died.

In the late 19th century, the Crow experienced constant pressure from missionaries, teachers, and government officials. With the buffalo gone, the tribe's Sioux and Blackfoot enemies confined to their own reservations, and the Northern Pacific running nearby, it seemed obvious to whites that the Indians should change and become more like their new non-Indian neighbors. However, the Crow did not see it that way. Just as they had allied themselves with the government during the Plains wars because they were trying to protect themselves, so they now accepted the government's agents and missionaries as necessary evils. And even though their children reported to government schools and tribal members attended church on Sunday in growing numbers, they continued the other features of their traditional way of life that had still survived unharmed.

Throughout this era of change, families continued to be a central feature of Crow life. Clans still banded the tribes-people together. The Crow retained their traditional religious beliefs, even though they had begun to adopt some Christian ones. Because of these threads to the past, the Crow continued to think of themselves as a distinct group. A high tide of change had come and swept away many familiar things, but the people and their sense of identity remained. ▲

Chief Two Leggings, in a portrait taken by photographer Edward S. Curtis in 1908.

THE
RESERVATION
ERA

During the summer of 1887, a 24-year-old man named Wraps Up His Tail faced a problem common to many other Crow Indians his age: How could a young warrior prove himself now that he could no longer go on buffalo hunts and raids against the Sioux? Wraps Up His Tail knew that it made sense for older Crow to maintain peace with non-Indians. By doing so, the tribe had been able to hold on to significant pieces of its Bighorn homeland. But the government agents acted as if the Crow had been defeated in war. They issued orders prohibiting the Indians from riding outside the reservation boundaries to look for game or journeying to the mountains in search of visions. The reservation provided safety from non-Indian settlers and miners, but it also seemed to wrap a young man's dreams in a binding of rules and regulations. To Wraps Up His Tail, the "wisdom" of his elders and the "order" of the res-

ervation had made it impossible to follow the Crow's traditional path to manhood.

Many other young Crow shared his unhappiness. He Knows His Coups, for example, was very proud of his father, Crazy Head. This chief had distinguished himself in battles against the Sioux and the Blackfoot and had served as a courier and scout for the soldiers at Fort Smith. Crazy Head was widely respected by the tribe for his accomplishments. Although He Knows His Coups wanted to follow in his father's footsteps, he could not because he had no way to demonstrate his own bravery and leadership abilities.

Frustrated with life at Crow Agency, Wraps Up His Tail, He Knows His Coups, and their friends were excited when a group of Northern Cheyenne from the Tongue River Reservation, which bordered the Crow's land, invited them to their annual Sun Dance.

The dance had been banned by the Crow's agents and had not been performed by the tribe for many years. These young Crow were therefore eager to take advantage of an opportunity to participate in the ceremony revered by their fathers and grandfathers.

During the Sun Dance, men underwent voluntary self-torture. They sometimes cut pieces of flesh from their body and offered them as a sacrifice to the tribe and as a plea for blessings from the Creator. Young men also punctured the muscles in their chests and looped rawhide strings under their skin through the holes. The strings were then tied to a pole, in front of which the men stood and leaned back until the rawhide was pulled tight. Eventually, the strings broke through the skin and set the young men free. By stoically enduring the intense pain of this ritual, Crow men had traditionally proved their bravery to other tribe members. Missionaries and government officials were horrified by the Sun Dance, but for young Crow it offered a chance to act like warriors.

At the Northern Cheyenne's ceremony, Wraps Up His Tail showed himself to be an especially brave man. The Cheyenne were so impressed by the young Crow that they offered him a saber and with it a new name—Sword Bearer. Sword Bearer's fame gave him a surge of confidence and optimism. He no longer wanted to accept the rules of non-Indians in stiff collars who shook their head in disgust at the tribe's sacred traditions. He was a Crow and a warrior. He was not meant to wear a school uniform or walk behind a plow.

Some elders in the tribe encouraged Sword Bearer's new outlook. Two such leaders, Crazy Head and Deaf Bull, had grown tired of the government's promises. Crazy Head's cattle had been stolen by local cowboys; the government did nothing but say it was sorry. Deaf Bull had asked Williamson for food and equipment, but the agent had refused. He told Deaf Bull to prove his worth by farming before expecting any assistance. These older Crow said to Sword Bearer that if he felt called to action then he should act. Following the white man's orders did not seem worth the effort.

Late in the summer of 1887, Sword Bearer led 22 men north to retaliate against a band of Blackfoot who had captured some of the Crow's horses. They had to cross more than one set of railroad tracks to get to the Blackfoot agency, but these dedicated warriors had determined that they would not allow any of the changes brought to the Plains by non-Indians to deter them from their raid. Although the Crow agent and the reservation police knew of Sword Bearer's plans, they did nothing to stop them. The young Crow men seemed to be acting wildly, but government employees did not want to force a confrontation.

One came anyway on September 30, when the group returned in triumph. In the old days, after a successful raid their fathers would have driven the captured ponies through the camp while singing victory songs and shooting their guns in the air. Sword Bearer did the same thing as he led his men through the sleepy town of Crow Agency, but instead of firing his rifle over his head, he shot into the agent's house and the town store.

Suddenly the young men's celebration appeared to be an uprising. As Sword Bearer and the other warriors rode off into the night, the Crow agent telegraphed his superiors in Washington and the army commander at nearby Fort Custer. He reported the incident

A Crow man undergoing voluntary self-torture, in a photograph posed by Edward S. Curtis in 1908. One end of a rawhide string is tied to the pole; the other is threaded through holes punctured in the flesh of the man's chest. This ritual was traditionally performed during the Sun Dance, a ceremony that was prohibited by government officials at the time this photograph was taken.

Crow prisoners arrested after the U.S. Army's battle with Sword Bearer and his followers on November 5, 1887.

and asked them to send troops to help protect the agency. The local missionaries became worried that the tribe was returning to its "heathen" ways, and the nearby newspapers began warning non-Indian settlers in Montana Territory to prepare for another Indian war.

For the next few weeks, Sword Bearer's notoriety grew. He and his followers retreated into the mountains. Many Crow believed that the young man had special powers and that perhaps he was a holy man. Rumors flew among non-Indians: They speculated that the dreaded Sioux would join the Crow warriors, or that Indians from Canada would ride to their rescue, or that all Crow were about to rebel. As tensions rose, U.S. Army troops began arriving from Fort Custer and the East. Many Crow then moved their tipis closer to the agency to demonstrate that they wished to stay neutral in any conflict that might follow.

Finally, on November 5, the army ordered the arrest of Sword Bearer and his men. The warriors put up some resistance, but the fighting was brief. When the shooting stopped, eight Crows, including Sword Bearer, had been killed.

With Sword Bearer's tragic death, the reservation era began. Although the Crow had lived on a reservation for decades, up until this time they had been able to retain a sense that the Crow world was limited only by the strength of a man's pony. Following the events of 1887, however, young men could no longer expect to participate in raiding parties and Sun Dances. Instead, they would have to prove their manhood and power in peaceful ways. Agents began to enforce their rules more firmly, and the Crow now felt the restraints of reservation life. People had to stay in one place. They had to buy their supplies with cash rather than through trade. They could no longer ignore missionaries and government officials.

But Sword Bearer's exciting life showed that old dreams lived on in a new setting. Young men still sought ways to prove themselves, and the Crow wanted to keep their traditions alive. The tribe had survived too much simply to give up their ways and live like white people.

Before the reservation was established, the Crow lived together in bands during the winter, but spent the rest of the year in smaller groups that traveled across the Plains hunting, raiding, and visiting with other Crow or Indian tribes. In the reservation era, they were forced by agency officials to find permanent homes. They settled in several different communities, which would from then on form the backbone of Crow social life. Yet even the Crow who grew up on the reservation still enjoyed moving from place to place and camping with special friends and relatives.

A number of River and Mountain Crow families settled along Pryor Creek in the western portion of the reservation. These Crow were led by Chief Plenty Coups as well as The Wet and Bell Rock, two men who had been prominent in the Fox warrior society during the years of conflict with the Sioux. Many of the residents of the Pryor community probably belonged to the Foxes or were in some way related to the three chiefs. Because Pryor was geographically far from Crow Agency, agents often had difficulty exerting their will over the people there.

About 30 miles to the east of Pryor was another Crow community. It was established in the Bighorn River valley

Portrait of Chief Pretty Eagle painted by E. A. Burbank. Although friendly to non-Indians, Pretty Eagle was so tough that one agency employee kept a loaded pistol nearby whenever the chief visited him.

near the former site of Fort Smith. In the early years of the reservation, Chief Iron Bull lived in the middle of the valley. Until his death shortly before the Sword Bearer incident, he had advocated that his Crow neighbors take up farming and convert to Christianity. When Father Prando first visited the Crow, he stayed with Iron Bull and established the St. Xavier mission close to the chief's home.

Chief Pretty Eagle lived farther up the valley near a place where he had a vision as a young man. Although friendly to non-Indians and willing to try his hand at farming and ranching, he was widely respected as a stubborn defender of his people. Pretty Eagle was so tough, in fact, that one agency employee said he kept a loaded pistol in his desk whenever the old man came by to discuss tribal business. Many of his comrades and his Mountain Crow relatives settled near him along the northern end of the Bighorn River.

Another community grew up on the rolling prairies to the south of the confluence of the Bighorn and Little Bighorn rivers. Here, near present-day Hardin, Montana, was Black Lodge, the principal settlement of the River Crow. This branch of the tribe had lived to the north of the Yellowstone River before the 1880s, when they decided to move south in order to take up homes closer to their Mountain Crow kin. Led by several chiefs, including Two Leggings and Two Belly, the River Crow continued to return to the old territory to hunt for as long as they could, but as the buffalo disappeared they soon had to rely on their farms or on the agency storehouse for their food. A U.S. Army post, Fort Custer, was in the center of Black Lodge. Some Crow worked for the soldiers there or sold them firewood.

Twelve miles to the south on the Little Bighorn River was Crow Agency. The settlement was essentially a government town; most of its residents

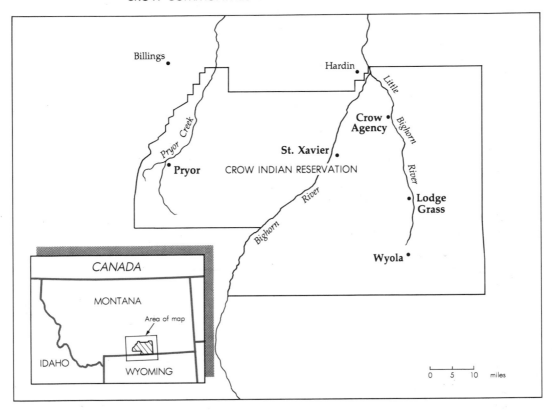

worked for the Bureau of Indian Affairs. In addition to the non-Indians it employed—the agent, office clerks, and schoolteachers—it hired dozens of Crow as agency policemen, as teamsters to transport goods from the railroad to the agency, and as teachers' aides, cooks, or janitors at the boarding schools. Although Crow Agency was founded by non-Indians, the majority of its population was made up of Crow Indians.

In the early 1900s another large reservation community grew up at the head of the Little Bighorn Valley near the site where Lodge Grass Creek flows into the Little Bighorn River. Like the Bighorn Canyon communities, the Lodge Grass settlement was established near a place where travelers could easily cross the Bighorn Mountains and journey south into Wind River country. The Crow had camped and hunted in this area for centuries.

Most of the Crow at Lodge Grass were members of Kicked in the Bellies, the branch of the tribe that had separated from the Mountain Crow in the 18th century. Among its most prominent early settlers were Medicine Crow,

Grey Bull, and Spotted Horse. In about 1900 some Lodge Grass residents moved about 10 miles south and founded another community, Wyola, near the source of the Little Bighorn River. The Crow in both Lodge Grass and Wyola became extremely influential in reservation affairs, in part because their geographical closeness to the agency made it easy for them to plead their case before government officials. In particular, Medicine Crow and his relatives carried great weight at tribal meetings. During the period the Crow were establishing these communities, the federal government once again pressured the tribe into selling part of its territory. In response to the demands of miners and ranchers for access to more land in the new state of Montana, the government in 1892 induced tribal leaders to agree to give up 1.8 million acres in the mountainous western portion of their reservation. In return, the Crow were to receive 50 cents per acre. During the negotiations, the tribe also managed to exact a number of promises from the government. Specifically, the United states agreed to build an irrigation system in the Bighorn River valley and to support the development of Indian cattle herds.

A view of the Crow Agency in about 1910.

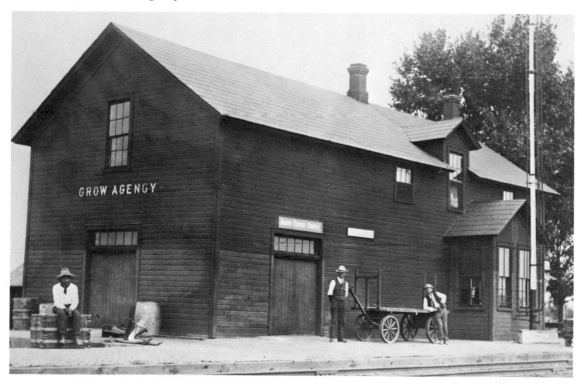

A Crow camp near the community of Lodge Grass.

A similar process unfolded in 1899 when government officials asked Crow leaders to approve the sale of nearly 1 million acres along the Yellowstone River, a large triangle of land that encompasses present-day Hardin, Montana. The tribe bargained hard, and the officials agreed to pay them $1.03 per acre. Congress, however, later rejected the land sale on the grounds that the Indians' price was too high. During the next several years, local white farmers and politicians increasingly demanded that more Crow land be opened for non-Indian settlement. Finally, in 1904 Montana senator Joseph M. Dixon persuaded his fellow lawmakers to ignore the 1899 agreement and set new terms for the sale. In the new agreement, the Crow lost 1 million acres of land and received far less than $1 million for it.

With the 1904 sale, the Crow reservation was reduced to its present size. Although the tribe had managed to hold onto its beloved Bighorn and Little Bighorn river valleys, the Crow were now owners of only an amputated remnant of their original homeland. Crow country had become a block of land with almost no natural boundaries surrounded by growing cities and ambitious non-Indian cattlemen and farmers.

In the early 1900s, another government policy threatened to undermine the unity of the Crow people. Following the enactment of the General Allotment Act by Congress in 1887, the federal government had begun to divide tribally owned reservation land throughout the United States into small plots, known as allotments. One allotment then became the private property of each Indian on the reservation. The government believed that if individual Indians owned land, they would have a greater incentive to farm and live like their non-Indian neighbors.

In preparation for allotting the Crow Indian Reservation, officials began in

A Crow family in their home, photographed in 1910 by an assistant clerk at the Crow Agency. After the tribe's land had been allotted, many Crow began to live in cabins rather than tipis.

the 1890s to survey the Crow lands. From that time (but more forcefully after 1904), they encouraged each Crow to select an area as his or her allotment and to build a home and farm there. The male head of each household received 160 acres; his wife, 80 acres; and each of his children, 40 acres. By choosing adjoining plots, a family could gain legal title to a sizable amount of land.

As the allotment process continued, more and more Crow began to build fences around their plots and to live in cabins that were separated from one another by considerable distances. Never-

theless, Crow families still kept in close contact. People often shared houses with relatives or lived in tents pitched in their brothers' or sisters' front yard. Even when family members lived in different homes, they visited one another regularly. Groups of friends who owned separate farms or ranches were always eager to stay in touch by working together. In the 1890s and the first decades of the 1900s, the government hired Crow to work on the Bighorn Valley irrigation project. These workers and their families camped together and spent their days carrying supplies.

Crow in different communities would take advantage of any reason to gather together and renew their ties. Every summer, groups left their homes and retreated into the Bighorn Mountains to gather berries and escape the heat of the prairie. In the fall and spring, the Tobacco Society held dances and initiation ceremonies. In the winter, teams from several settlements challenged each other at the hand game, a traditional Crow contest requiring great manual skill. Each team included men and women who sang and drummed to express their support for their players. Large crowds watched these spectacles and bet on the games' outcome. Throughout the year, communities looked for opportunities to get together to dance and sing. (In addition to each settlement's groups of singers, the Crow had several organizations, such as the Nighthawk Singers and the Hot Dancers, that recruited members from different communities and had a large following throughout the reservation.) The Crow also assembled in large camps to celebrate holidays, such

A 1930s photograph of Crow men playing the hand game, a sleight-of-hand contest that is still popular with the tribe.

as Christmas or the Fourth of July. Non-Indians who witnessed these gatherings usually assumed that the tribe was extremely religious or patriotic. But the Crow themselves considered these holidays little more than an excuse to camp and feast together.

In 1904 the Crow agent decided to organize an annual tribal gathering that would be sponsored by the government. He wanted to hold a fall agricultural fair where Crow could be rewarded for their farming and household achievements. At the fair, the Crow could show their farm products and compete for prizes in canning, sewing, and baking. Most Crow disliked the idea of a farm show, but they welcomed the chance for a get-together, even at the risk of getting caught in a fall snowstorm en route. Over the years, however, the tribe gradually changed the event by introducing their own fair activities, including parades, horse racing, dancing, and Tobacco Society meetings.

The Crow Fair is just one example of the many efforts made by government agents during the reservation era to change the tribe's traditions. Often these changes were forced on the Crow. They were prohibited from leaving the reservation without their agent's permission and were not allowed to practice many of their traditional religious rituals. If the Indians defied these rules, they were persecuted or jailed. The agents succeeded in stopping some large group activities, but religious rituals conducted by smaller gatherings of

people, such as the ceremony held by the Tobacco Society to adopt new members, and by individuals, such as vision quests, continued. The non-Indians in charge of the reservation assumed that the Crow were stupid or backward when the Indians refused to behave in a "civilized" fashion. They did not realize that the Crow just wanted to continue their old ways.

The missionaries on the Crow reservation were equally intolerant of the Crow's traditions. At the start of the reservation era, Father Prando had dreamed of persuading all of the Crow to give up their ancestors' beliefs and convert to Christianity. (In one of his early letters, the priest had said that someday he would "turn the Crows into doves.") Soon after Father Prando had established the Catholic church at St. Xavier in 1887, many other churchmen with the same goal came to live and preach among the Crow. In 1891, Congregationalist minister James Gregor Burgess founded a Protestant mission at Crow Agency. Twelve years later, Baptist missionaries opened a church at Lodge Grass. By the beginning of World War I, the Baptists were operating several day schools along the Bighorn River and in the Wyota community, and Catholic missions had been established at Lodge Grass and Pryor. The Congregationalists spread their influence to Black Lodge, but following the death of Burgess in 1919 their numbers declined. In 1921 all of their churches among the Crow became affiliated with the Baptists. By 1930

A women's horse race held at one of the first Crow Fairs.

Catholic and Protestant churches had been established in all communities on the Crow reservation.

During the period these Christian churches were founded, the Crow were introduced to another new religion. Early in the 20th century, tribes in Oklahoma began using peyote, a variety of cactus native to Mexico and the lower Rio Grande Valley, as a sacrament in a religious ceremony that combined elements of Christianity and traditional Indian beliefs. The Southern Cheyenne embraced this new faith and passed it on to their kin, the Northern Cheyenne on the Tongue River Reservation. News of the peyote meetings they began to hold in the 1910s quickly spread to their Crow neighbors. Soon government officials at Crow Agency reported to their superiors that the Crow in the Lodge Grass and Bighorn communities were performing the peyote ritual.

These Crow would hold their all-night peyote meetings in tents erected near their homes. Men usually led the ritual, but many women participated. During these meetings, people consumed pieces of the peyote plant and then sang and prayed until sunrise. Ingesting the peyote plant stimulated visions for many believers and was seen as a means of establishing contact with spiritual power. The long peyote ritual created an intimate bond among its participants, and the peyote plant gave them a way of communicating with God. By 1940, peyote meetings were performed by a broad cross section of the tribe, including both educated young people and elders, and were taking place throughout the reservation.

During the reservation era, there was also a revival of traditional Crow religious practices. Government officials tried to stop the Crow from performing their old ceremonies, but leaders such as Medicine Crow and Plenty Coups defended the tribe's beliefs by insisting that they harmed no one. Throughout the 1920s, Tobacco Society chapters in Lodge Grass, Pryor, and Bighorn continued to meet and cultivate their ceremonial tobacco gardens. Every summer, members brought new people into the society by adopting them in a formal ceremony. Throughout the winter, the chapters met to instruct these new members in the society's rituals and songs. As membership increased, so did the strength of the bonds of friendship and family among the Crow who belonged to the Tobacco Society.

By the time the United States entered World War II in 1941, there were many paths a Crow could take to heaven. Within each community, there were Protestants, Catholics, followers of the Peyote religion, and Crow whose religious beliefs were the same as their ancestors'. All of these religions were practiced openly, and none dominated the others. Because the Crow continued to speak their own language, maintain a strong sense of family, and believe in their traditions, they could tolerate new faiths without seeing them as a threat to their tribal identity.

The Crow also came to accept new criteria for selecting their chiefs. As Sword Bearer's death in 1887 made apparent, the traditional Crow methods of choosing tribal leaders were out of date. In the reservation era more than ever, a Crow leader needed skill in dealing with non-Indians, the loyal following of his community, and an excellent sense of when to be tough and when to retreat in a disagreement with the government.

The first leader to distinguish himself in the reservation era was Plenty Coups. Throughout his later life, he often told his followers about a vision he had as a young man in which a storm destroyed all of the trees in a dark forest except for one. The remaining tree was the home of a chickadee, a tiny bird known for its bright-eyed observation of the world around it. The chief believed that the Crow would survive the onslaught of non-Indian settlers only if they, like the chickadee, were constantly vigilant. Plenty Coups himself was cautious, a quality he demonstrated by refusing to join Sword Bearer in his defiance of the government. But he was also a dedicated leader who was always determined to help his people.

A Mountain Crow descended from Long Hair—the chief who signed the tribe's 1825 treaty—Plenty Coups lived in Pryor and operated a trading post there. His home was a center of activity in the western portion of the reservation. Relatives and friends could always count on the chief to give them a meal or loan them money. As Plenty Coups grew older, he also began to entertain non-Indian tourists.

Plenty Coups's ease in dealing with non-Indians helped him get his way when he had disputes with government officials. As a young man, he had been a member of the delegation that traveled to Washington to negotiate the Crow's 1880 land cession. Because of this experience and several return trips to the capital the chief usually had much better connections in the East than the Crow's agents did.

The marriage of a Crow couple performed in 1900 by Protestant missionary James Gregor Burgess, who had founded a mission at Crow Agency in 1891.

Chief Plenty Coups, 1905.

Plenty Coups was able to use his influence in Washington effectively because he understood the workings of the federal government. For instance, he knew that non-Indians belonged to two different political parties and that, although the commissioner of Indian affairs made the federal policies that affected the Crow, Congress was responsible for appropriating government money to the tribe. If Plenty Coups did not like a particular policy, he discovered that the political opponents of the policymaker would be eager to listen to his complaints. He also found that when the Crow publically said that they had been cheated by their agent or local white merchants, officials in the Baptist or Catholic church might come to the Indians' defense. When the tribe had a problem, the chief would call on churchmen if he felt they would sympathize with his cause.

As Plenty Coups grew older, he became better known in Washington. (In fact, when the tomb of the unknown soldier was dedicated in Arlington National Cemetery in 1921, the War Department chose Plenty Coups to represent all American Indians at the ceremony.) He also became increasingly independent. If officials at Crow Agency embarked on a program that he disliked, the chief would simply refuse to cooperate or would complain directly to one of his contacts in the capital.

Throughout his life, Plenty Coups displayed an understanding of the non-Indian world but kept a place in his own. Although he became a Catholic, he continued to be active in the Crow Tobacco Society and to enjoy dancing at ceremonies. He joined the local Kiwanis club and preached the importance of education, but he was ready to demand the dismissal of any reservation schoolteacher who he believed was cruel or incompetent. He cooperated with the tribal police force, but he resisted the government's efforts to dictate Crow behavior. After Plenty Coups's death in 1932, he was recognized as the last traditional chief of the Crow. He had imitated the chickadee successfully and had helped his people survive the continuing storm of change. Both the Crow and non-Indians in eastern Montana today honor the chief by preserving his home as a museum and a park.

The second leader to dominate the politics of the reservation era was Robert Yellowtail. Born in the mid-1880s just as his people were relocated permanently to the valley of the Little Bighorn River, Yellowtail was a member of the first generation of Crow who spent their entire life within the confines of the reservation. Yellowtail and his contemporaries were educated at government schools and were exposed to Christianity at an early age. He was fluent in both Crow and English and felt as comfortable in Washington, D.C., and Billings, Montana, as he was herding cattle and horses on his ranch near Lodge Grass.

In the early 20th century, Yellowtail and other young, educated Crow gained importance in the tribe as advisers to chiefs such as Plenty Coups, Medicine Crow, Holds the Enemy, and Spotted Rabbit. These older leaders knew little English. When they went to Washington, their advisers—Yellowtail, Richard Wallace, Joe Cooper, Russell White Bear, and Arnold Costa, among others—accompanied them to translate and speak on their behalf. In 1911 the U.S. government allowed the Crow to establish a Business Committee composed of elected representatives to be the voice of the tribe in all official dealings. This group quickly became dominated by these "school boys."

During the 1920s, the Crow gradually replaced the Business Committee with a general council, in which all the members of the tribe met to transact business. At first, tribe members simply gathered to watch the Business Committee meetings, but as interest in these deliberations grew, the audience became more powerful than the elected delegates. By 1930 the general council, led by a small steering committee, had become the Crow's official tribal government. The council was a freewheeling, democratic body that decided all questions by majority vote. It was extremely unpopular with U.S. government officials, who criticized its inefficiency, but it was a wonderful arena for emerging tribal politicians such as Yellowtail, Russell White Bear, and George Washington Hogan. By the end of the 1920s, Yellowtail and his political allies were usually able to dominate the council by using favors, family ties, and moving speeches to induce the majority of the council to vote for the causes they supported.

In 1934 the commissioner of Indian affairs selected Robert Yellowtail as the Crow reservation's superintendent, the title by which the Bureau of Indian Affairs had referred to agents since 1908. After more than a century of official contact with the tribe, the U.S. government had at last appointed a Crow to be in charge of tribal affairs. This event was widely celebrated on the reservation. It marked the start of a new era in which the tribe would be able to speak for itself and chart its own course in American history.

The tribe quickly demonstrated its willingness to go its own way when in 1935 it rejected the Indian Reorganization Act, a government plan that would

A family traveling to the 1941 Crow Fair, where William Big Day led the tribe's first Sun Dance since the 1880s.

have allowed the Crow to write a constitution under federal supervision. John Collier, a visionary new commisioner of Indian affairs who had been appointed to his job by President Franklin D. Roosevelt, urged the tribe to accept the new law. However, the Crow's suspicion of the federal government ran deep. They overwhelmingly voted down the new law in a special referendum. The tribe wanted to continue making decisions at its general council.

Although the Crow continued to live on a reservation, the reservation era and the oppression associated with it essentially ended in 1934 because the Crow were no longer governed by outsiders. They were freer now to pursue

the religion of their choice, to travel and visit as they pleased, and to enjoy their clan and village traditions without fear of criticism or interference. The Crow were still a minority in Montana, but they had weathered the influx of non-Indian outsiders by finding ways of balancing the "Indian" and "modern" worlds. Like the lone tree in Plenty Coups's vision, they had survived the storm and still stood tall.

In 1938, 51 years after Sword Bearer's death, another Crow man left the reservation to attend a Sun Dance. William Big Day, who had grown up in Pryor, was indifferent to the lessons of his schoolteachers and priests but curious about his tribe's culture and history. During the 1920s he had attended peyote meetings and had even tried to re-create a vision quest. Like Sword Bearer, Big Day yearned to discover a way to establish an identity that was authentically Crow and free from the influence of non-Indians.

That summer he and his wife decided to visit the Shoshone Sun Dance, which was held every year at the Wind River Reservation in Wyoming. As the drumming and singing began, Big Day thought that the Sun Dance songs sounded familiar even though he had never attended the ceremony before. He suddenly realized that he had heard the songs in his dreams. These songs, his dreams had told him, would make all Crow people happy. Big Day and his wife were thrilled by their experience in Wyoming and returned to Wind River to participate in the ceremony again the next year. Big Day then began to receive instruction from a Shoshone religious leader in how to conduct the ceremony himself.

In 1941 Big Day felt ready to hold a Sun Dance near his home at Pryor. He won immediate approval for the idea from Superintendent Yellowtail and quick support from his clan relatives. The dance was performed in June and was repeated in August at the Crow Fair.

Thus, a new version of the ceremony that had been the springboard for fighting and death in 1887 was greeted as an occasion for celebration only slightly more than 50 years later. The success of William Big Day's Sun Dance proved that the Crow's interest in their Indian culture had survived the reservation era. Once again the ceremony gave the Crow a sense of great power, even though it now took place in a world of cars and cameras that Sword Bearer could never have imagined. ▲

A boy at the Crow Fair in 1983.

7

THE
CROW
TODAY

Today more than 8,000 people live on the Crow Indian Reservation, the boundaries of which have remained the same for nearly a century. Unlike a century ago, however, reservation residents are not all members of the tribe. About a third of the reservation population is made up of non-Indians who have purchased or leased land from the Crow. Also, about 1,000 Crow live in nearby towns and cities, such as Hardin and Billings. Most of these off-reservation Crow commute "home" on weekends or for special events. Pryor, St. Xavier, Lodge Grass, and Crow Agency continue to be the reservation's principal population centers but community ties have grown somewhat looser than they were in the early decades of the 20th century.

Many Crow are now employed by the tribal government, which has grown dramatically since World War II owing to an increase in the funds it receives from Washington. Money from the federal government has been used to establish several different social programs, including ones aimed at the improvement of health care, education, and housing for the reservation population. The tribal government hires Crow to work as managers and other personnel to administer these programs. It also employs tribespeople as social workers and reservation policemen.

Other Crow find jobs at the local community college and with coal-mining companies. The Little Bighorn Community College employs Crow as teachers and support staff. These instructors supplement the school's standard curriculum with special programs on tribal history and language and with courses that prepare Crow students for careers in their own community. Dozens of Crow are equipment operators, clerks, and supervisors for companies

One of the dozens of Crow Indians employed by the mining companies with operations on the tribe's reservation.

that mine coal on the reservation. These firms pay the tribal government a fixed amount of money for every ton of coal they extract from areas where the tribe owns the subsurface minerals.

Some tribespeople commute to jobs in Hardin, the seat of Bighorn County, which encompasses the Crow Indian Reservation. Since the early 1900s, Crow have worked for their non-Indian neighbors there as cowboys, waitresses, and farmhands.

Nevertheless, there have frequently been periods when Crow could not find work. The unemployment rate among the Crow has sometimes zoomed to above 50 percent. In recent years, this has posed a particular problem because fewer tribespeople now plant gardens or raise cattle for their food than in the past. When Crow cannot find work, they, like other unemployed Americans, suffer greatly without money to buy groceries and other necessities, such as gasoline and clothes.

Past leaders such as Plenty Coups and Robert Yellowtail had always hoped that the Crow on the reservation would be able to support themselves by farming and ranching. Unfortunately this has not become a reality for several reasons. First, the Crow have never had enough money to operate their farms and ranches properly. A farmer needs seed and fertilizer. A rancher has to have cattle. Both require special tools and some training in order to be able to perform their jobs. They also need a large enough savings to support themselves during the occasional year when a farmer's harvest is small or a rancher cannot get a good price for his beef. Although the federal government has often supplied some Crow with tools and cattle, the members of the tribe have not had access to the same resources as non-Indian farmers and ranchers. Crow have not been able to borrow money from local banks to get them through hard times or to afford the agricultural training available to non-Indians at Montana's technical schools and universities. Even when the government did try to help the Crow with supplies, the Indians were usually still at a disadvantage. For instance, unlike their non-Indian neighbors, they could not choose their own tools, but had to use whatever their agent gave them.

Second, most Crow have not succeeded as farmers and ranchers because non-Indians have always pressured the Indians to sell their lands. When a Crow becomes discouraged or uninterested in farming, there is usually someone nearby who would like to rent or purchase his or her property. When the U.S. government divided the Crow reservation into individually owned plots in the late 19th century, officials would not allow the Crow to sell their land without permission. They thought Indians would not be able to manage their own property. Beginning in the 1920s, however, many of these restrictions were lifted. In recent years, the government has given Crow individuals the option of selling their land on the open market. Even those Crow who have decided to keep their land now usually let someone else rent or manage it for an annual fee. Thus, although the Crow have had few incentives to farm and ranch in competition with non-Indians, the ensured income from selling or leasing their land has provided them with

Two Crow cowboys on a ranch near Crow Agency. In the distance is the site of the Battle of Little Bighorn.

a good reason to give control of their property to someone else.

Third, many Crow have mixed feelings about farming and ranching. Although they are eager to be financially independent, they are not always willing to commit themselves to one activity at the expense of all others. Today, as they were centuries ago, Crow are very concerned about their families and involved in their communities. With these priorities, they are usually more hesitant than non-Indians to devote themselves to these time-consuming ways of making a living. Crow often feel that, if a relative needs help or a community activity needs organizing, the chores of running a farm or taking care of cattle might just have to wait.

Finally, Crow leaders have been effective in preventing non-Indians from cheating tribespeople out of their property, but they have not always been successful managers of the tribe's resources. Inexperienced, untrained, and outnumbered by business rivals in non-Indian communities, Crow politicians have not been able to develop successful tribal businesses. The general council has remained the central decision-making body on the reservation. Although very democratic, this organization has hampered politicians' efforts to put long-range projects into motion and to pursue important, but unpopular, goals.

Robert Yellowtail, who died in 1988, was the tribe's elder statesman for many years, but other men and women who followed him have also had success eliciting the support of the majority at council meetings. Prominent among this younger generation have been Frank Takes Gun, who became a leader in the Native American Church, and Edison Real Bird, who presided over the expansion of tribal services and programs in the 1960s.

Despite their economic hardships, the Crow have maintained the rich social and cultural life they created early in the reservation era. The Tobacco Society continues to adopt new members and to hold meetings, dances, and ceremonies year-round. Each summer, the Crow perform several Sun Dances, which attract visitors from other reservations as well as many tribe members. Throughout the fall and winter, hand game players from different communities compete with each other. A championship hand game contest ends the long season of community rivalry.

The high point of the Crow's social calendar is the annual Crow Fair, which is now held during the third weekend in August. The scene of reunions of Crow families and friends, the fair has featured a full program of parades, Indian dancing, rodeo riding, and horse racing since the 1930s. Perhaps the fair's greatest attraction is the display of hundreds of tipis erected in two giant circles on the outskirts of Crow Agency. For four days each year, the Crow boast that their reservation is the "tipi capital of the world." Thousands of Indian and non-Indian tourists arrive from Oklahoma, California, Illinois, and states further east to see these events.

The Crow continue to practice several different religions. A number of evangelical churches have become popular since World War II, and gospel meetings have increasingly competed with Tobacco Society ceremonies and Sun Dances for the attention of the reservation population. But regardless of their faith, all Crow still place a great importance on their spiritual life and treasure their religious organizations.

As in earlier times, tribal values and traditional beliefs are observed in an atmosphere of change. Although the Crow have made a great effort to maintain clan and community loyalties, new stresses in their life have worked against these attempts. Economic problems have hurt isolated communities, especially Pryor. In hard times, the immediate concerns of individuals become more important, making it more difficult for extended families and clans to maintain a sense of unity. Reservation schools have failed to deal sensitively with Crow children; many have

Robert Yellowtail, who died in 1988, was the tribe's elder statesman for more than 50 years.

lost interest in their education, dropped out of school, or fallen behind in their studies. Alcohol-related problems on the reservation have also magnified these other pressures. Churches, clans, and communities are all working to overcome these problems, but their task is sometimes overwhelmingly difficult.

As the Crow prepare to enter the 21st century, they feel great pride in their ancient culture as well as in their recent history. They have experienced tremendous changes in their life but nevertheless they have been able to keep many of their traditions alive. Their determination to defend their beliefs and themselves remains firm.

Today most of the Crow's battles take place in the courtroom, but, as in the past, the tribe's future still depends on how successfully the Crow fight their enemies. In the 1980s, the Crow emerged as victors when they went to court to change the way the Bighorn

Bill Yellowtail, son of Robert Yellowtail, who was elected to the Montana state senate.

A procession of dancers at the 1980 Crow Fair.

County runs its government. A young Crow woman named Janine Pease Windy Boy and a number of other tribal members proved that the county government and its employees had discriminated against several Crow. They demanded that each member of the board of county commissioners—the chief decision-making body in the local government—should be elected by a single district. This system would ensure the presence of at least a few Crow on the board. A federal judge agreed with the tribe's representatives. The new system of electing commissioners has opened the door to greater participation by the Crow in county affairs.

The Crow have also won the right to try some cases in their own tribal court. Today disputes that arise between two parties on the reservation must be argued in this court if one of the participants is a Crow. Tribal courts also handle disagreements between members of the tribe. These cases involve issues ranging from adoption to traffic violations and are decided by a judge who is elected by the Crow.

Elvis Old Bull (right), of the Lodge Grass High School Indians, leads his team to victory in the 1989 Montana state high school basketball championship.

In recent times the tribe has had some success in blocking policies established by Congress and the Montana legislature. For instance, in 1988 the Crow prevented the state government's attempt to block a tribal tax on the coal-mining companies that operate on the reservation. The tribe also defeated both the state and the federal government's effort to outlaw the use of peyote in religious rituals. The Crow's triumphs in these battles have reassured the tribe that laws and judges can be helpful allies in the struggle to defend their traditions.

Courtroom battles have not always ended in victories for the Crow, however. In the 1950s the Crow were not able to stop the U.S. government from building a dam across the Bighorn River. Although the project produced jobs and a new source of electric power for eastern Montana, it flooded the beautiful Bighorn Canyon and destroyed many areas where Crow had camped and prayed in the past. It was a bittersweet day when the government announced that the new dam would be named in honor of Robert Yellowtail, who had fought the project from the beginning.

With the Crow's traditional love for competition and ceremony, it should not be surprising that some of the loudest (and most enjoyable) battles now fought between the Crow and their neighbors take place on the basketball court. Together the teams of the high schools in Lodge Grass and Pryor have won several state basketball titles. These victories have been a great source of community pride. As grandparents, clan uncles, and other relatives gather to cheer the young "warriors," fans from surrounding towns get a glimpse of the fierceness and loyalty for which the Crow have been known throughout their history. The state finals held in midwinter are now as much a part of the Crow's annual calendar as the hand game championships and the adoption rituals of the Tobacco Society.

Since their creation from a handful of earth and their migration to the Great Plains, the Crow have remained loyal to each other and defended themselves against enemies of all stripes. They have suffered great hardships, but they have also won great victories. The spring that has driven them forward through bright days and times of darkness has always been their belief in themselves. This belief cannot be changed by new laws or winter storms or hard times. It survives in the people, the descendants of Eelapuash, Iron Bull, and Plenty Coups, who call themselves Absaroka. ▲

BIBLIOGRAPHY

Beckwourth, James. *The Life and Adventures of James P. Beckwourth*. Lincoln: University of Nebraska Press, 1972.

Bernardis, Tim. *Baleeisbaalichiwee History: Teacher's Guide*. Crow Agency, MO: Bilingual Materials Development Center, 1986.

Brown, Mark. *Plainsmen of the Yellowstone*. Lincoln: University of Nebraska Press, 1961.

Denig, Edwin Thompson. *Five Indian Tribes of the Upper Missouri: Sioux, Arikaras, Assiniboines, Crees, Crows*. Edited by John C. Ewers. Norman: University of Oklahoma Press, 1961.

Frey, Rodney. *The World of the Crow Indians: As Driftwood Lodges*. Norman: University of Oklahoma Press, 1987.

Linderman, Frank. *Plenty Coups: Chief of the Crows*. Lincoln: University of Nebraska Press, 1962.

————. *Pretty Shield: Medicine Woman of the Crows*. Lincoln: University of Nebraska Press, 1974.

Lowie, Robert H. *The Crow Indians*. Lincoln: University of Nebraska Press, 1983.

McGinnis, Dale K., and Floyd W. Sharrock. *The Crow People*. Phoenix, AZ: Indian Tribal Series, 1972.

Nabokov, Peter. *Two Leggings: The Making of a Crow Warrior*. Lincoln: Unveristy of Nebraska Press, 1982.

Vogel, Fred W. *The Shoshoni-Crow Sundance*. Norman: University of Oklahoma Press, 1985.

Wood, W. Raymond, and Thomas D. Thiesson, eds. *Early Fur Trade on the Northern Plains*. Norman: University of Oklahoma Press, 1985.

THE CROW AT A GLANCE

TRIBE *Crow*

CULTURE AREA *Great Plains*

TRADITIONAL GEOGRAPHY *Montana, Wyoming, and western North and South Dakota*

LINGUISTIC FAMILY *Siouan*

CURRENT POPULATION *approximately 8,000*

FIRST CONTACT *probably François Antoine Larocque, French, 1805*

FEDERAL STATUS *recognized. Most Crow live on the Crow Indian Reservation in Montana, although some reside in the nearby towns of Billings and Hardin.*

Absarokee The name the Crow call themselves; literally, "children of the long-beaked bird." Early explorers believed that this bird was a crow, thereby giving the tribe the name by which it is now best known.

agent A person appointed by the Bureau of Indian Affairs to supervise U.S. government programs on a reservation and/or in a specific region. After 1908 the title *superintendent* replaced *agent*.

agriculture Intensive cultivation of tracts of land, sometimes using draft animals and heavy plowing equipment. Agriculture requires a largely nonnomadic way of life.

allotment U.S. policy applied nationwide through the General Allotment Act passed in 1887, aimed at breaking up tribally owned reservations by assigning individual farms and ranches to Indians. Allotment was intended as much to discourage traditional communal activities as to encourage private farming and assimilate Indians into mainstream American life.

anthropology The study of the physical, social, and historical characteristics of human beings.

archaeology The recovery and reconstruction of human ways of life through the study of material culture (including tools, clothing, and food and human remains).

Awatixa One of the three divisions of the Hidatsa tribe. The Crow trace their ancestry to the Awatixa, who migrated to what is now North Dakota in the 17th century and became hunters on the Great Plains.

bacheeitche The Crow word for "chief," which literally means "good man." Crow leaders were granted power according to their moral and ethical standing among the tribe members.

band A loosely organized group of people who are bound together by the need for food and defense, by family ties, and/or by other common interests.

bate Crow word for male tribe members who preferred to live as women. Such individuals were thought by the Crow to have special ties to the Creator.

breechcloth A strip of animal skin or cloth that is drawn between the legs and hung from a belt tied around the waist.

Bureau of Indian Affairs (BIA) A U.S. government agency now within the Department of the Interior. Originally intended to manage trade and other relations with Indians, the BIA now seeks to develop and implement programs that encourage Indians to manage their own affairs and to improve their educational opportunities and general social and economic well-being.

clan A multigenerational group having a shared identity, organization, and property based on belief in descent from a common ancestor. Because clan members consider themselves closely related, marriage within a clan is strictly prohibited. The Crow word for clan, *ashmmaleaxia*, literally means "driftwood lodges."

culture The learned behavior of humans; nonbiological, socially taught activities; the way of life of a group of people.

Great Plains A flat, dry region in central North America between the western edge of the Great Lakes region and the Rocky Mountains that was covered by lush grasslands at the time of American settlement in the 19th century.

Hidatsa An Indian tribe of the northern Great Plains. The Hidatsa were active middlemen in a trade network between Europeans and Plains Indian tribes and are ancient relatives of the Crow.

Ice Age A time in the earth's past when vast ice sheets, or glaciers, in the Arctic and Antarctic expanded to cover much of North America and Eurasia. The most recent Ice Age (Pleistocene) began about 18,000 years ago.

Jesuit A member of the Society of Jesus, a Roman Catholic order founded by Saint Ignatius Loyola in 1534. The Jesuits are highly learned and in the 17th century were particularly active in spreading Christianity outside Europe.

medicine bundle An animal-skin pouch containing objects of spiritual power, usually those seen by their owners in a vision.

mission A religious center founded by advocates of a particular denomination who are trying to convert nonbelievers to their faith.

Mountain Crow One of the two major divisions of the Crow tribe. There were two groups of Mountain Crow in the 19th century: the "Main Body," who lived near the Bighorn Mountains, and the "Kicked in the Bellies," who inhabited the valleys of the Little Bighorn and Powder rivers.

peyote A cactus plant that is native to Texas, New Mexico, Arizona, and the northern Mexican states. The fruit, or buttons, of the cactus are sometimes ingested to enhance or channel prayer in many American Indian religious ceremonies, particularly those of the Native American Church.

reservation, reserve A tract of land retained by Indians for their own occupation and use. *Reservation* is used to describe such lands in the United States; *reserve,* in Canada.

River Crow One of the two major divisions of the Crow tribe. The River Crow lived along the upper reaches of the Missouri River and maintained strong ties with their Hidatsa relatives.

Sun Dance The annual religious and cultural renewal ceremony of the Crow and other Indian nations. While many Plains Indian tribes held Sun Dances to instill general feelings of confidence and power in the members of the tribe, the Crow traditionally performed these ceremonies specifically to avenge the killing of relatives or close friends in battle.

territory A defined region of the United States that is not, but may become a state. The government officials of a territory are appointed by the president, but territory residents elect their own legislature.

tipi A conical, portable shelter made of poles and traditionally covered with animal hides; by the mid-19th century the hides were replaced by canvas sheets. Tipis were the principal dwelling of most Plains Indians during much of the 18th and 19th centuries.

treaty A contract negotiated between representatives of the United States government or another national government and one or more Indian tribes. Treaties dealt with the cessation of military action, the surrender of political independence, the establishment of boundaries, terms of land sales, and related matters.

tribe A society consisting of several or many separate communities united by kinship, culture, and language, and other social institutions including clans, religious organizations, and warrior societies.

vision quest A fast and vigil undertaken by Indian youths in the hope of receiving a sign from a supernatural power who might guide and protect them throughout their life. The vigil usually required a person to stay outdoors alone for an extended period of time.

PICTURE CREDITS

The American Heritage Center, The University of Wyoming, page 86; American Museum of Natural History, Department of Library Services, pages 22 (Photo by Charles H. Coles, neg.# 319386), 44 (Photo by Robert H. Lowie, neg.# 118859); Wayne Arnst, page 118; Bancroft Library, University of California, Berkeley, page 15; The Charles H. Barstow Collection of Indian Ledger Art, Eastern Montana College Library, Special Collections, pages 38, 60; The Bettmann Archive, page 55; The British Museum, page 26; Photo by Elsa Spier Byron, Courtesy of the Museum of the Rockies, pages 99, 101; Michael Crummet, pages 112, 113, 116; Courtesy of Sally Curtis, page 105; The Denver Art Museum, pages 42, 50; The Field Museum of Natural History, Chicago, cover, pages 73–81; Bob Hawks, page 110; Harley Hettick, pages 115, 117; The Joslyn Art Museum, pages 25, 56; Library of Congress, pages 34, 45, 66, 90, 93, 96, 108; The Montana Historical Society, Helena, page 88; Museum of the American Indian/Heye Foundation, pages 63, 71, 98; National Anthropological Archives, Smithsonian Institution, pages 30 (neg.# 3436-H), 41 (neg.# 79-8487), 46 (neg.# PL-742883), 51 (neg.# PL-45186), 72 (neg.# 56,560), 87 (neg.# 3421-b-7), 100 (neg.# 4644), 103 (neg.# 56,264), 106 (neg.# 3405); The National Archives, pages 70, 94; National Museum of American Art, Smithsonian Institution, Gift of Mrs. Joseph Harrison Jr., pages 12, 20, 23, 32, 48; The Newberry Library, page 64; Courtesy of the New-York Historical Society, page 16; The New York Public Library, Rare Books and Manuscripts Division, page 57; The State Historical Society of North Dakota, pages 58, 69; H. H. Tammen Collection, The Colorado Historical Society, page 84; The U.S. Geological Survey, page 18; Walters Art Gallery, page 61.

Maps (pages 2, 29, 53, 83) by Gary Tong.

ACKNOWLEDGEMENTS

In preparing this book I have drawn upon the special skills of a number of people. Stephen Weston Hoskins generously offered his editorial and stylistic advice, Mardell Hogan Plainfeather checked my descriptions of Crow social structure, and both Tim Bernardis and Peter Nabokov reviewed the manuscript for accuracy and wording. Throughout this effort, I have been encouraged and sustained by colleagues in both Montana and Chicago, especially Joseph Medicine Crow, Eloise Whitebear Pease, and Father Peter Powell. I am grateful for all of this assistance, but I remain responsible for any imperfections that may remain in the text.

FREDERICK E. HOXIE is director of the D'Arcy McNickle Center for the History of the American Indian at the Newberry Library in Chicago. He holds a B.A. from Amherst College and a Ph.D. in history from Brandeis University. Dr. Hoxie is the author of several books, including *A Final Promise: The Campaign to Assimilate the Indians, 1880–1920* (1984), and editor of *Indians in American History: An Introduction* (1988). He is a former associate professor of history at Antioch College.

FRANK W. PORTER III, general editor of INDIANS OF NORTH AMERICA, is director of the Chelsea House Foundation for American Indian Studies. He holds a B.A., M.A., and Ph.D. from the University of Maryland. He has done extensive research concerning the Indians of Maryland and Delaware and is the author of numerous articles on their history, archaeology, geography, and ethnography. He was formerly director of the Maryland Commission on Indian Affairs and American Indian Research and Resource Institute, Gettysburg, Pennsylvania, and he has received grants from the Delaware Humanities Forum, the Maryland Committee for the Humanities, the Ford Foundation, and the National Endowment for the Humanities, among others. Dr. Porter is the author of *The Bureau of Indian Affairs* in the Chelsea House KNOW YOUR GOVERNMENT series.